AN

INTRODUCTION

TO

THE HISTORY AND STUDY

OF

CHESS;

WITH

Copious Descriptions,

Etymological & Practical;

TOGETHER WITH

A SYSTEM OF ELEMENTARY RULES

FOR PLAYING:

TO WHICH IS ADDED,

THE ANALYSIS OF CHESS

OF

ANDRÉ DANICAN PHILIDOR.

The whole simplifyed, and arranged in a manner entirely new,

BY AN AMATEUR.

Of armies on the chequer'd field array'd,
And guiltless war in pleasing form display'd,
When two bold kings contend with vain alarms,
In iv'ry this—and that in ebon arms,
Sing, sportive maids, that haunt the sacred hill
Of Pindus, and the fam'd Piërian rill.
Caïssa, by SIR WILLIAM JONES.

Cheltenham,

PRINTED BY H. RUFF:

FOR DWYER, NO. 29, HOLBORN HILL; ROBINSONS, AND
HURST, PATER-NOSTER ROW; RICHARDSON, ROYAL
EXCHANGE; GINGER, PICCADILLY; CARPENTER,
AND FAULDER, BOND STREET: AND H. RUFF,
AND S. HARWARD, CHELTENHAM.
1804.

PREFACE.

AMIDST all the amusements that
have been invented by man, for the
employment of the idle, or the relief
of the studious, Chess stands *unique*
and pre-eminent. It is indisputably
the noblest of games, and worthy
the attention, as it has been the enthusiastic delight, of the greatest
characters, whether kings, warriors,
or philosophers. Many of the latter
have rank'd it among the Sciences,
and Mr. Philidor elegantly says,
" Its pursuit is almost unremittingly
productive of problems, not unworthy the solution of genius; and

whose extent and intricacy elude even the *suspicion* of ordinary minds."

As an amusement it possesses one advantage as great as it is singular. It is so highly interesting in itself, and the attention is so strongly engaged by it, that it requires not the additional inducement of gain, and in consequence is rarely or never played for money.

It must be acknowledged, however, that in proportion as the attention is kept up, so are the passions aroused, and the chagrin and disappointment considerable on being defeated; since as chance has nothing to do in the decision, and *ill luck*, therefore, cannot be blamed, the player experiences all those sensations that naturally arise from defeat occasioned by misconduct. A specific against these may be found in the admirable little Treatise on the " Morals of Chess," by Dr. Franklin, contained in the 6th Chapter, Page 85, where he holds out to the loser the power of gaining a victory, equally difficult, but, it must be confessed, much more honourable.

The object of the Editor has been to collect and comprise in one volume, as well the *history* as the *tactics* of the game. With respect to the former point, he acknowledges himself indebted to a publication in 2 vols. printed in 1787 and 1789, being a collection of whatever has appeared on the subject in any other book, either domestic or foreign. Where he has had access to the originals, he has consulted them; where not, he has freely transcribed. These

volumes are purely *theoretical*; the
quotations appear to follow as they
occurred to the Compiler, and method and arrangement seem equally
unaimed at and unattained.   Most,
if not all, of the other modern publications are as purely *practical*; so
that the principal view of the Editor
remains unimpeded by any other
Work.   In the Etymological Description of the Pieces, &c. he is
greatly indebted to the ingenious
paper transmitted to the Antiquarian
Society by Francis Douce, Esq.

Feeling that originality on this
subject was, in a great degree, impossible, the Editor has endeavoured
to keep in view, on all occasions,
those explanations and elucidations,
which are *desiderata* to the learner:
this will be evident throughout.—

From the same motive, he has taken pains so to new model and arrange the Rules for playing, that instead of being unconnected, and consequently in a great degree incoherent, as hitherto, they will be found to compose an uniform system, which will supply to the learner the place of a great portion of, otherwise unavoidable, practice; and he presumes with confidence that a serious attention to them, supported by a diligent study of the Analysis, will as speedily form a good player, as the delicate combinations and intricacies of this first of games will permit.

CONTENTS.

CHAPTER I.

HISTORICAL SKETCH OF THE PROBABLE ORIGIN AND PROGRESS OF THE GAME OF CHESS.

CHAP. II. *Page* 15.

OF THE POWERFUL EFFECTS OF CHESS ON THE MIND AND PASSIONS.

b

CHAP. III. 31.

OF THE DIFFERENT MODES OF PLAYING, AND THE VA-
RIOUS PIECES, &c. THAT HAVE BEEN USED.

CHAP. IV. 51.

OF CHESS PLAYERS, AND PUBLICATIONS ON CHESS.

CHAP. V. 62.

ETYMOLOGICAL DESCRIPTION OF THE GAME, PIECES, &c.
AND EXPLANATION OF THE TERMS MADE USE OF.

CHAP. IX. 139.

PRACTICAL EXAMPLES, INTRODUCTORY TO PHILIDOR'S
ANALYSIS.

PHILIDOR's ANALYSIS. 161.

CHESS.

CHAPTER I.

HISTORICAL SKETCH OF THE PROBABLE ORIGIN AND PROGRESS OF THE GAME OF CHESS.

THE origin of Chess still remains a matter of dispute; of its high antiquity, however, there rests no doubt.

Some give the invention of it to Palamedes, during the siege of Troy (near twelve centuries before Christ); who endeavoured, by its introduction, to prevent that irksomeness amongst the Greeks, which the length of the siege threatened to render intolerable. But even allowing him to have been the inventor of a game at that period, it is not certain that the modern Chess has any great affinity to it.

B

Others imagine it had its origin in China, and Mr. Irwin, in a letter from Canton to the Earl of Charlemont, gives him the following translation from the *Concum*, or *Chinese Annals*, respecting the invention of the game, as delivered to him by Tinqua, a soldier mandarin, of the province of Fokien.

" Three hundred and seventy-nine years after the time of Confucius, or one thousand nine hundred and sixty-five years ago, Hung Cochu, King of Kiangnan, sent an expedition into the Shensi country, under the command of a mandarin, called Hansing, to conquer it. After one successful campaign, the soldiers were put into winter-quarters ; where, finding the weather much colder than what they had been accustomed to, and being also deprived of their wives and families, the army in general became impatient of their situation, and clamorous to return home.

" Hansing, upon this circumstance, revolved in his mind the bad consequences of complying with their wishes. The necessity of soothing his troops, and reconciling them to their position, appeared urgent, in order to finish his operations the ensuing year. He was a man of genius, as well as a good scholar; and having contemplated some time on the subject, he invented the game of Chess, as well for the amusement of his men, in their vacant hours, as to inflame their military ardour, the game being wholly founded on the principles of war. The stratagem succeeded to his wish. The soldiery were delighted with the game; and forgot, in their daily contests for victory, the inconveniences of their post. In the spring the general took the field again; and in a few months, added the rich country of Shensi to the kingdom of Kiangnan, by the defeat and capture of its king, Choupayuen, a famous warrior among the Chinese. On this conquest Hung Cochu assumed the title of Emperor, and Choupayuen put an end to his own life in despair."

The manner of playing I shall give hereafter, when I treat of the various modes in use.

Mr. Irwin infers, that the game is probably of Chinese origin, from the following:—

" That the confined situation and powers
of the king, resembling those of a monarch
in the earlier .parts of the world, .counte-
nance this supposition ; and that, as it
travelled. westward, and descended to
later times, the sovereign prerogative ex-
tended .itself, until it became unlimited, as
in our state of the game. That the agency
of the. princes, in lieu of the queen, be-
speaks .forcibly the nature of the Chinese
customs, which exclude females from all
power or influence whatever; which princes,
in its passage through Persia, were changed
into a single. vizier, or minister of state,
with the large portion of delegated authority that exists there; instead of whom, the
European nations, with their usual gallantry,
adopted a queen on their board. That on
the acquisition of so strong a piece as the
vizier, the *paö*, or rocket boys, were sup-
pressed, as possessing powers unintelligible,
at that time, to other nations, and three
pawns added in consequence to make up the
number of men ; and that, as discipline im-
proved, the lines, which are straggling on
the Chinese board, might have been closed.

on ours. That the river between the parties is expressive of the general face of this country, where a battle could hardly be fought without encountering an interruption of this kind, which the soldier was here taught to overcome; but that, on the introduction of the game into Persia, the board changed with the dry nature of the region, and the contest was decided on *terra firma**. And lastly, that in no account of Chess that he had seen has the story been so consistent or characteristic as the above." With the Indians (according to him) it was designed by a Brahmin, to cure the melancholy of the daughter of a rajah. " But with the Chinese, it was invented by an experienced soldier, on the principles of war. Not to dispel love-sick vapours, or to instruct a female in a science that could neither benefit nor inform her; but to quiet the murmurs of a discontented soldiery; to employ their vacant hours in lessons on the military art,

---

* This reasoning will be better understood, when the description of the Chinese game, in the third chapter, is read.

and to cherish the spirit of conquest in the bosom of winter quarters. Its age is traced by them on record near two centuries before the Christian æra; and among the numerous claims for this noble invention, that of the Chinese, who call it, by way of distinction, *Chong Kè,* or the *Royal Game,* appears alone to be indisputable."

Others again suppose it originated in India; and the story adopted by these is as follows:

It is said, that about the beginning of the fifth century of the Christian æra, there was in the Indies a very powerful prince, who took to himself the proud title of King of the Indies; his father had forced a great number of sovereign princes to pay tribute to him, and submit themselves under his empire. The young monarch, not aware that kings ought to be the fathers of their people; that the subjects' love of their king is the only solid support of his throne; and that a king without subjects would only bear an empty title, without having any real superiority over others, fell into the most unbounded licentiousness and cruelty.

His priests and nobility. in vain represented to him the impolicy of his conduct,
but intoxicated with the idea of his gran-
deur, which he thought was not to be shaken,
he despised their wise remonstrances ; and,
on their complaints and representations continuing, he to revenge his authority, which
he thought despised by those who thus dared
to disapprove his conduct, caused several
of the chief of them to be put to death by
the most cruel torments.

This affrighted the others; they were
silent : and the prince abandoned to himself,
and, what was far more dangerous for him,
and terrible to his people, given up to the
pernicious counsels of flatterers, was hurried
on to the last excesses. The people were
oppressed under the weight of this tyranny ;
and the tributary princes, persuaded that
the king of the Indies, in losing the love of
his people had lost the very essence of his
power and strength, were preparing to throw
off the yoke.

Then a Brahmin, or Indian philosopher,
named Nassir (Serses, or Sissa), the son
of Daher, touched with the misfortunes

of his country, undertook to make the
prince open his eyes upon the fatal effects which his conduct was likely to produce; and sensible his lesson would not
prove of any service, until the prince should
himself make the application of it, he invented the game of Chess, where the king,
although the most considerable of all the
pieces, is impotent both to attack and defend himself against his enemies, without
the assistance of his subjects and soldiers.

The new game soon became famous; the
King of the Indies heard of it, and would
learn it. The Brahmin Nassir was called
upon to teach it him, and, under the pretext
of explaining the rules of the game, and
shewing him the necessity of the other
pieces for the king's defence, he made him
perceive and relish important truths, which
he had hitherto refused to hear. The king,
endued naturally with understanding and
virtuous sentiments, which even the pernicious maxims of his flatterers and courtiers
could not wholly extinguish, was struck
with the Brahmin's lessons; and, convinced
that in the people's love of their king con-

sisted all his strength, he altered. his conduct, and prevented the misfortunes that
threatened him.

The story adds, that the prince, sensible
of the great service rendered him, left to
the Brahmin himself the naming of his re-
ward, who desired that the number of grains
of corn might be given him the chess-board
would produce, reckoning one for the first
square, two for the second, four for the
third, and so on, doubling always to the
sixty-fourth.

The King's astonishment, at the seeming
moderation of the demand, was only exceeded by his learning, after he had willingly
granted it, that all the treasures of his vast
dominions would be insufficient to satisfy it.
Then the Brahmin laid hold of this oppor-
nity to give him an additional lesson on the
importance it was to kings to be upon their
guard against those who are about them,
and how much they ought to be afraid of
their ministers abusing their best intentions.

The remarks of Mr. Irwin, on the Chinese story, are ingenious; and, perhaps, it will,
in the opinion of most persons, be deemed

more probable than the Indian one; I shall only add, that as the latter is said to have arisen some centuries after the former, the Brahmin Nassir may only have copied instead of invented.

Others say, it was invented by two Grecian brothers, named Lydo and Tyrrheno. Who being afflicted with great hunger, in order not to feel it so much, passed their time in playing at this game.

The author of a little book printed in 1685, says, Chess was invented in the year 3635, by a certain wise man named Xerxes, to shew to a tyrant, that majesty and authority, without strength and assistance, without the help of men and subjects, was obnoxious to many calamities; which is, perhaps, only a confusion of the Indian story.

The game of Chess, wherever it arose, was not long confined there, but soon passed into Persia. The Persians looking upon it as a game to be made use of in all countries, to instruct kings at the same time that it amused them, gave it the name of *Schertrengi,* or *Schatrak;* the *game of schah,* or *king.* And also that of *Sedrentz,* or *Hundred Cares.*

Fabricus says, that a celebrated Persian astronomer, named Schatrenscha, was the inventor; and that from him it derived its name.

From the Persians it passed to the Arabians, who introduced it into Spain; and it was brought into England during the reign of William the Conqueror, who was himself a great player, and is said to have lost several lordships in Lincolnshire and elsewhere at it.

The first western authors who have mentioned Chess, are the old French romancers, or the writers of those fabulous histories of the Knights of the Round Table, King Arthur's brave Courtiers, of the Twelve Peers of France, and of the Palatines of the Emperor Charlemagne.

Those who wish to dive more deeply into the origin of Chess, and its connexion with, or deviation from, the most ancient games, may peruse a work, published by Becket, 1801, in quarto, intitled, " An Inquiry into the ancient Greek Game, supposed to have been invented by Palamedes," where they will find the subject treated in a masterly manner, and as fully elucidated as the remoteness of its antiquity will permit.

There are few countries at present where it is not known and played.

Mr. Coxe, who was in Russia in 1772, says, " Chess is so common in Russia, that during our continuance at Moscow, I scarcely entered into any company where parties were not engaged in that diversion ; and I very frequently observed in my passage through the streets, the tradesmen and common people playing it before the doors of their shops or houses. The Russians are esteemed great proficients in Chess. With them the queen has, in addition to the other moves, that of the knight, which, according to Philidor, spoils the game, but which certainly renders it more complicated and difficult, and of course more interesting. The Russians have also another method of playing at Chess, namely, with four persons at the same time, two against two ; and for this purpose, the board is larger than usual, contains more men, and is provided with a greater number of squares. I was informed that this method was more difficult, but far more agreeable than the common game."

The Danes were early fond of Chess and dice, for Bishop Etheric, coming to Canute the Great about midnight upon urgent business, found the King and his courtiers engaged at play; some at dice, and others at Chess.

Chess has from a very early period been a favourite game among the inhabitants of Iceland; many of whom, particularly those who inhabit the western part of that island, are at this day very skilful players, peasants as well as gentlemen. The same rules which are observed in other countries, are with very few exceptions followed here; the words and phrases in the game are those which were adopted by the ancient Norwegians.

It is a custom among the most illustrious Goths and Swedes, when they intend to marry their daughters, to prove the disposition of the suitors that come to them, and to know their passions, especially by playing with them at tables, or Chess. For at these games, the passions and motions of their minds, and the forces and properties of their fortunes are used to be seen:

as whether the wooer be rudely disposed,
that he will indiscreetly rejoice, and sud-
denly triumph when he wins; or whether,
when he is wronged he can patiently and
wisely endure it.

It is much practised in Barbary, and also
in the kingdoms of Fez and Morocco.

CHAP. II.

OF THE POWERFUL EFFECTS OF CHESS ON THE MIND AND PASSIONS.

———

THE great interest taken in this warlike game—the importance attached to a victory —and the disgrace attending defeat, are exemplified in numerous instances handed down to us by various writers, of which the most worthy of notice are the following.

The *Anatomy of Melancholy* * says,—

———

* This extraordinary book, this heterogeneous mass of learned quotations, which long slept in obscurity on old book stalls, unless occasionally rescued by curiosity for the trifling sum of one shilling, was brought into public notice and admiration by a paper read to the Philosophical Society of Manchester, January 21, 1791, (*see Vol. IV. p. 4 of their Transactions*), by Dr. Ferriar ; in which he clearly proves, that to this book Sterne owes much of his apparently original humour. The price, which before seldom exceeded half-a-crown, now rose to one guinea and one guinea and a half, if the copy was in good condition, and bound in the usual stile of

William the Conqueror, in his younger
years, playing at Chess with the Prince of
France (Dauphiny was not annexed to that
Crown in those days,) losing a mate, knocked
the chess-board about his pate, which was
a cause afterwards of much enmity betwixt
them.

King John was playing at Chess when
the deputies from Rouen came to acquaint
him that their city was besieged, but

---

modern elegance. Commerce, ever on the watch, soon
occasioned an edition to be published in 2 vols. 8vo. but
so great was the public curiosity become, and such the
rapid demand, that the whole was speedily taken off,
and in the meantime the original editions scarcely sunk
in value a moment. The book was published under
the signature of *Democritus Junior*. It was first printed
in quarto, afterwards in folio in 1624, 1628, 1632, 1638,
1651, and 1652; and it is said the bookseller got a fortune by it. The author having foretold his own death,
was strongly suspected of causing it himself rather than
that his prophecy should be belied.

The public seems to catch at a circumstance of this
kind; and for the same reason, *The Divine Weeks and
Works of Du Bartas*, from which it is supposed Milton
freely drew, has experienced a similar, though not an
equal rise.

he would not hear them until he had finished his game.

Charles I. was also playing at it when news was brought of the resolution of the Scots to sell him to the English ; but so little was he discomposed by this alarming intelligence, that he continued his game with the utmost composure.

In a battle between the French and English, in the year 1117, an English knight seizing the bridle of Louis le Gros, and crying to his comrades, " the King is taken !" the Prince struck him to the ground with his sword, saying " *Ne sçais tu pas qu' aux echecs on ne prend pas le roi ?*"—" Dost thou not know that at chess the king is never taken?" The meaning of which is, that at the game of Chess, when the king is reduced to that pass, that there is no way for him to escape, the game ends ; because the royal piece is not to be exposed to an imaginary affront.

John Frederic, Elector of Saxony, was, in 1547, taken prisoner by the Emperor Charles V. and condemned to suffer death by being beheaded.

This decree was intimated to the Elec-

tor while amusing himself at playing at
Chess with Ernest of Brunswick, his fellow-
prisoner. He paused for a moment, though
without discovering any symptom either of
surprise or terror; and after taking notice
of the irregularity, as well as the injustice of
the Emperor's proceedings; " It is easy, continued he, to comprehend his scheme. I
must die, because Wittemberg will not surrender; and I shall lay down my life with
pleasure, if, by that sacrifice, I can preserve
the dignity of my house, and transmit to
my posterity the inheritance which belongs
to them. Would to God, that this sentence
may not affect my wife and children more
than it intimidates me! and that they, for
the sake of adding a few days to a life already too long, may not renounce honours
and territories which they were born to possess!" He then turned to his antagonist,
whom he challenged to continue the game.
He played with his usual attention and in-
genuity, and having beat Ernest, expressed
all the satisfaction which is commonly felt
on gaining such victories. After this he
withdrew to his own apartment, that he

might employ the rest of his time in such religious exercises as were proper in his situation.

Carrera says, " That either ravished with the delight of the game, or armed with his usual fortitude and magnanimity, he heard the news with such an intrepid mind, and without any symptom of fear, that he immediately anew invited the Duke to play.

Gregorio Leti, in his Life of Charles V. says, " After the Elector had heard his sentence, he turned to a page in waiting, and, without testifying any emotion, ordered him to bring a chess-board, and immediately began to play with the Duke of Brunswick, and appeared delighted with having won two games.

He was not, however, put to death; for in 1552, before Charles left Inspruck he withdrew the guards placed on the degraded Elector, whom, during five years, he had carried about with him as a prisoner, and set him entirely at liberty.

In this case the Elector owed neither his life nor his liberty to his playing at Chess; but the following proves that there has been at least one who was indebted to the interest he took in it, not only for his life, but the possession of a crown added to it.

In the Chronicle of the Moorish Kings of Grenada, it is related, that, in 1396, Mehmed Balba seized upon the throne, in prejudice of his elder brother, and passed his life in one continued round of disasters. His wars with Castile were invariably unsuccessful; and he fell at last a victim to poison. Finding his end approaching, he dispatched an officer to the fort of Solobrena, to put his brother Juzaf to death, lest that Prince's adherents should form any obstacle to his son's succession. The Alcayde found the Prince playing at Chess. Juzaf begged hard for two hours' respite, which was denied him. The officer however at length permitted him to go on with his game; but before it was finished, a messenger arrived with the news of the death of Mehmed, and the unanimous election of Juzaf to the crown.

Seneca tells a story of one Canius Julius, who was playing at Chess (*ludebat latrunculis*), at the time that a centurion, who led

a troop of condemned men to death, commanded him likewise to be cited. Having
scarcely finished his game, he counted his
men, and said to him with whom he played,
" Beware when I am dead that thou be-
liest me not, and sayest thou hast won the
game." Then nodding his head to the centurion, he added, " Bear me witness, that I
have the advantage of one."

Al Amin, Khalif of Bagdad, and his freed-
man Kuthar, were playing at chess without
the least consideration of impending danger,
when his brother Al Mamun's forces pushed
the siege of Bagdad with so much vigor,
that the city was upon the point of being
carried by assault, and the Khalif himself
was obliged to fly: it is said, that he cried
out, when warned of his danger, " Let me
alone! for I see check-mate against Kuthar."

When Charles XII. was at Bender, Vol-
taire says, " for his only amusement he
played sometimes at Chess." It is not uncommon for such a man's character to be
more developped by little circumstances
than by those of greater consequence ; it
may be mentioned, therefore, that he brought

out the king early, and by making use of it more than any of the other pieces, he generally lost the game. When he was besieged by the Turks, in the house in which he had shut himself up, near Bender, after he had well barricadoed it, he sat down coolly to play at Chess with his favourite, Grothusen, as if every thing had been in profound security.

Ferrand, Count of Flanders, having been taken prisoner by Philip Augustus at the battle of Bovines, his wife, who might have obtained his release, left him to languish a long time in prison. They hated each other, and their hatred proceeded from playing at Chess together: the husband could never forgive his wife for constantly beating him; and she never could resolve to suffer him to win a game.

Col. Stewart, who had been aid-de-camp to the Earl of Stair, and was afterwards one of the Quarter-masters General in the Duke of Cumberland's time, used frequently to play with the Earl, who was very fond of the game; but an unexpected check-mate used to put his Lordship into such a passion,

that he was ready to throw a candlestick, or
any thing else that was near him, at his adversary ; the prudent Colonel always took
care therefore, to be on his feet, to fly to the
farthest corner of the room, when he said,
" check-mate, my Lord !"

The following anecdote, though not
strictly according with the nature of the
preceding, deserves a place for its singular-
ity. It is to be found in the *Introduction
to Cunningham's History of Great Britain.*
" When Lórd Sunderland was at the Hague,
he contracted a particular intimacy with
Mr. Cunningham, as they were both remarkable Chess-players. Whenever his
Lordship was at leisure, he either drove to
Cunningham's lodgings, which were at some
distance, or sent his carriage for him. After
playing for a course of time, Lord Sunderland discovered, that he who was jolted in
the carriage before they sat down, was always sure to lose every game : for which
reason, he gave over going to Cunningham's, but always sent for him, and always
beat him, to his no small astonishment, as
he was conscious that he understood the

game as well as his adversary. At last, when he was very much out of humour, Lord Sunderland told him the trick, and Cunningham insisted, that they should drive to one another's lodgings alternately, which confirmed his Lordship's observation, and restored Cunningham to his former level; for, from that time, they won and lost alternately.

" This fact, which appears not at all incredible, for the streets of the Hague were not, in the last century, so smooth as those of London are at present, proves how nicely the capacities of Sunderland and Cunningham were balanced against each other."

The writer of this paragraph seems to think, that the head of a chess-player, before he plays, must be moved as carefully as a bottle of old port, before it be decanted.

While Mr. Cunningham resided at the Hague, a German Prince, hearing of his great skill in the game of chess, came to that city with a view of playing with him at that truly noble amusement. The Prince, whose name is not mentioned, informed Mr. Cunningham, by a note, of the purpose of his coming to the Hague. Mr. Ogilvie, laird of Cluny, a Scotch gentleman, in the Dutch service, who passed with many for little better than an ingenious madman, happened to be with Mr. Cunningham, when he received the note, to whom he said, "that he did not chuse to risk his reputation, for the knowledge of the game of Chess, with a person whom he did not know; and wished, that Cluny would go and play a game or two with the prince, in the character of one of Mr. Cunningham's disciples." Cluny agreed to go; and Mr. Cunningham is said to have written to the Prince to this purpose—that although he had the honour of receiving his highness's invitation to play a game at Chess with him, he could not accept of that honour, as business of a particular nature would not permit him at that time; but rather than his highness should be disappointed, he had sent one of his scholars to give him some entertainment that evening: and that, if his scholar should be beaten, he would do himself the honour of waiting on him (the prince) next day, and would play with him as many games as he should chuse.

Cluny accordingly went, and beat the prince
every game they played. Early next morn-
ing, the prince left the Hague, sensible,
that if he was shamefully defeated by the
scholar, he had, if possible, still less chance
of success with the master.

This story will not appear incredible, or,
indeed, anywise extraordinary, if we re-
flect on the high estimation in which the
game was held in the last century throughout all Europe.

It is said, that Dr. Franklin and the late
Sir John Pringle used frequently to play at
Chess together; and towards the end of the
game, the physician discovered, that the
velocity of his own as well as his adversary's
pulse was considerably increased. And Mr.
Twiss being requested to insert the circumstance in his book, seems to give it credi-
bility.

Richlêt, in his Dictionary, article *Echec*,
writes, " It is said, that the Devil, in order
to make poor Job lose his patience, had
only to engage him at a game at Chess."

The Spaniards say, that the game of
Chess is of use *para deflegmár un hombre;*

which may be translated, *to dephlegmatize a man.*

The practice of the Turks is worthy of imitation. Though fond of the game, and very expert at it, they play with great coolness, and testify neither joy at winning nor sorrow at losing, and yet they take such delight in playing, that they will pass whole days in so doing.

I shall add to this remark, and conclude these anecdotes, by mentioning, to the honour of Tamerlane the Great the Mogul Emperor, that though so attached to the game as to have named his fourth son, Shâh Rokh, from his having received the news of the birth of that prince while playing at Chess, and just as he had made the move so called, which is when the rook has given check, he was always rather pleased than hurt with the victory of a subject! an encomium, which the poorest Chess-player will know how to appreciate.

Lord Harvey, in the *Craftsman*, says, " Chess is the only game, perhaps, which is played at for nothing; and yet warms the blood and brain as much as if the

gamesters were contending for the deepest
stakes.   No person easily forgives himself
who loses, though to a superior player.
No person is ever known to flatter at this
game, by underplaying himself. It is certain, this play is an exercise of the understanding.   It is a contention, who has
the most solid brain ; who can lay the deepest and wisest designs.   It is, therefore,
rarely known, that a person of great viva-
city and quickness, or one of very slow
parts, is a master of this game."

And the editors of the *Gentleman's Maga-
zine* for July 1789, make this observation :
" We will venture to assert, that after ma-
thematics, logic; arithmetic, and one or two
other sciences, we are not acquainted with
any thing that more strengthens the mind
than Chess.   Were it possible to know that
two men were of exactly equal powers, natural and acquired, in every other respect
but with regard to Chess ; and if A could
play well at Chess, and B could not, A,
we should see (could we see such things)
would checkmate B, in every profession,
and every situation in life where they were

opposed. It is not a trifle to be accustomed to turn and twist one's mind to the shifting combinations of thirty-two men, with six different movements, on sixty-four squares. Lord Chatham, upon being complimented on one of his finest strokes in politics, is reported to have said, that " he deserved little praise, for his success arose only from having been checkmated by discovery, the day before, at Chess."

In the Critical Review for September, 1787, is the following passage: " The enthusiastic admiration of Chess-players for their game, is easily accounted for by those who have felt its influence, and have known the uncommon hold it takes of the mind and its affections. Equal players labour with great earnestness ; and a casual absence of mind alone determines the game. We have heard of a lady's suffering herself to be undressed, without perceiving it, while immersed in the mysterious movements of queens, bishops, and knights."

A pamphlet, intitled *A Letter to a young Gentleman just entered at the University*, published at Oxford in 1784, has this paragraph:

" Chess, by my advice, you will always
continue to practise. If we should meet
when you are some years older, I will tell
you the various reasons which I have for
advising you to play at this game, in preference to any game that depends only on
chance. Remember too, that after having
been able to learn Chess, you must not
complain of an inability to learn any thing
. else."

This extreme interest in the game renders
the playing for money unusual, as well as
unnecessary. M. de Legalle, however, the
instructor of Philidor, used to win half a
crown a game of the Chancellor d'Aguesseau,
and his scholar would frequently find persons to play with him at a crown a game;
but it may be supposed the object of such
persons was instruction, and not money.

Hoyle also taught how to open the game,
at a crown a lesson.

CHAP. III.

OF THE DIFFERENT MODES OF PLAYING,
AND THE VARIOUS PIECES, &c.
THAT HAVE BEEN USED.

I⊤ is most probable, that the game of
Chess, from whatever or whomsoever it
arose, was not originally as it is now played.
The great length of time that has elapsed
since its invention—the different countries
it has passed through—and the different
people who have used it, and felt more than
a common interest in it, seem to warrant
this idea.

The ancient games were played with peb-
bles, and perhaps upon the bare ground,
marked and scored for the purpose. Im-
provement was natural. Each nation might
add what it conceived to be such; and,
jealous of its perfection, reject what it might
fancy unnecessary innovations.

Many Europeans have invented games,

pieces, and moves, which they have flattered themselves have, by adding intricacy to difficulty, increased the satisfaction of playing; but the game, as it at present stands, seems to approach so nearly to perfection that that alteration may be considered the worst that recedes farthest from it.

The game played by the Chinese, called *Chong Kè*, and which, from the situation of the country, and the never-fluctuating manners of that people, may be supposed to have the greatest affinity to the original one, is as follows :—

There are nine pieces instead of eight to occupy the rear rank, and they stand on the lines between, and not within, the squares. The game is consequently played on the lines.

The king, or *Chong*, stands in the middle of this row. His moves resemble those of our king, but are confined to a fortress marked out for him.

The two princes, or *Sou*, stand on each side of him, and have equal powers and limits.

The mandarins, or *Tchong*, answer to our

bishops, and have the same moves, except that they cannot cross the white space in the centre of the board, (representing a river) to annoy the enemy, but stand on the defensive.

The knights, or rather horses, called *Maã*, stand and move like ours in every respect.

The war chariots, or *Tchè*, resemble our rooks or castles.

The rocket-boys, or *Paö*, are pieces whose motions and powers were unknown to us. They act with the direction of a rocket, and can take none of their adversary's men that have not a piece or pawn intervening*. To defend the men from this attack it is necessary to open the line between, either to take off the check on the king, or to save a man from being captured by the *Paö*. Their operation is, otherwise, like that of the rook. Their stations are marked between the pieces and pawns.

---

* This circumstance seems to add no little strength to the opinion entertained by many, that the invention of gunpowder originated with the Chinese, although the European invention, some centuries afterwards, might have been independant of it.

D

The five pawns, or *Ping*, make up the number of men equal to that of our board. Instead of taking sideways, like ours, they have the rook's motion, except that it is limited to one step, and is not retrograde. Another important point, in which the *Ping* differ from ours, is, that they continue in *statu quo* after reaching their adversary's head-quarters. It will appear, however, that the Chinese pieces far exceed the proportion of ours, which occasions the whole force of the contest to fall on them; and thereby precludes the beauty and variety of our game, when reduced to a struggle between the pawns, who are capable of the highest promotion, and often change the fortune of the day. The posts of the *Ping* are marked in front.

The Asiatic and African chess-boards are of a single colour, divided into squares: and indeed the distinction of colours, though it facilitates the playing, is otherwise superfluous.

Tamerlane's chess-board was eleven squares in breadth, and twelve in height.

In India, one of their games has 60 men

or pieces, and the movements are proportionably various.

The Germans sometimes play with a double chess-board, being two others placed laterally. There are two players on each side; each of whom, not only defends his own game, but joins his ally in more offensive operations.

There is a method of playing at Chess, called *Curzier-spiel*, at Stroepke, a village between Magdeberg and Brunswick, on a board of eight squares by twelve.

This village holds its lands upon the tenure of forfeiture, if any one of their community loses a game at Chess. Some of the inhabitants are expert at this play, but as the stake is so high, they decline finishing a game with a stranger, and defer the party *sine die.*

·· The oldest book written on Chess, before A. D. 1200, by *Jacopo Dacciesole,* or *Jacobus de Cæsollis,* intitled *De Moribus Hominum et Officiis Nobilium,* has the following prints of a set of chess-men.

The king on a throne, with a crown on

his head, the sceptre in his right hand, and a globe in his left.

The queen on a chair, with a mantle of ermine.

L'Alphine, a man sitting on a chair with an open book in his hand, representing a lawyer; as there are two of these pieces in the game, the book says, that he on the white square is for civil, and he on the black one for criminal cases. The knights, horse-men, armed *cap-à-pied.* The rooks, legates or vicars, men on horseback totally unarmed.

The first pawn, which stands before the king's rook, is a husbandman, with his bill in his right hand, and in the left a wand, to guide his oxen and flocks, and a pruning knife at his girdle.

The second pawn, placed before the king's knight, is a smith, with a hammer in one hand and a trowel in the other, clothed in a seaman's jacket.

The king's bishop's pawn is a man with a pair of sheers in one hand, a knife in the other, an inkstand hanging at his button, and a pen stuck behind his right ear.

The king's pawn has a pair of scales in

his right hand, in his left a measuring wand, and a purse of money hanging at his waist-band.

The queen's pawn is a man seated in an armed chair, with a book in one hand, and in the other a vial; various chirurgical in-struments are stuck in his girdle. This per-sonage represents a physician, who to be perfect, as the book says, ought to be a grammarian, logician, rhetorician, astro-loger, arithmetician, geometrician, and mu-sician.

The queen bishop's pawn is a man stand-ing at his own door, with a glass of wine in one hand, a loaf of bread in the other, and a bunch of keys at his girdle, represent-ing an inn-keeper.

The queen's knight's pawn, with two large keys in one hand, a pair of compasses in the other, and an open purse at his waist.

The eighth and last pawn is a man with his hair dishevelled, ragged cloaths, four dice in his right hand, a crust of bread in his left, and a letter pouch suspended from his shoulders.

Though I have given this description at

length from its curiosity, being the first
published, yet I much doubt whether such
a set ever existed, and whether the whole is
not to be considered, as Mr. Douce suggests,
an allegory or moralization, in which that
age delighted.

The following is an account of a set of
chess-men used at the Court of Denmark:
The kings and queens were dressed in their
robes, and seated upon thrones. The bishops
had their mitres and habits, richly adorned;
and the knights were mounted on horses, with
fine trappings. The rooks were elephants,
with towers on their backs. The men were
musketeers, presenting their guns close to
their cheeks, as if expecting the word to fire.

In the royal treasury of St. Denis, near
Paris, are kept some chess-men, with which
it is said Charlemagne (who died in 814),*
used to play. Only fifteen pieces and one
pawn are remaining, all of ivory, yellowed
by time; at the bottom of every one is an
Arabic inscription, which, according to Dr.

---

* This proves to a demonstration the game being near
1000 years old at least.

Hyde, is only the maker's name. The largest piece represents a king sitting on a throne, about twelve inches high, and eight broad, very clumsily carved: the other pieces are of so rude a form that it is difficult to say what they were intended to represent. The pawn (about three inches in height) is the image of a dwarf with a large shield ; the countenance is marked with a kind of ludicrous expression.

Dr. Hyde says, that Lewis the XIIIth of France had a chess-board quilted with wool, the men each with a point at the bottom ; by which means he played when riding in a carriage, sticking the men in the cushion.

Chess-boards are now commonly made for the use of those who travel by water, or in a carriage, with a hole in each square, a peg at the bottom of every man, and fifteen holes on each side of the board to hold the prisoners.

Charles I. had an elegant set of chess-men, which were kept in a magnificent bag. They are now in the possession of Lord Barrington. The chess-board is inlaid with ebony and ivory, of which materials the pieces are likewise made. The kings and queens are whole-length human figures, representing European and African sovereigns.

In 1747 there was at Rotterdam, in the possession of a coffee-house-keeper, a set of chess-men, which were made for Prince Eugene. They were three inches in height, of solid silver, chased; not different in colour, but sufficiently distinguished, by one party representing an European, and the other an Asiatic army.

A most valuable set of chess-men are also preserved at Rotterdam, which were made by Vander Werf, the celebrated painter, who employed the leisure hours of eighteen years in carving them. The pieces are three inches high, and the pawns two; half the number are of box, and the other half of ebony; they are all, except the castles, busts on pedestals. The kings are decorated with a lion's skin, of which the paws are crossed on their breast. The fools (bishops with us) have caps and bells, and are represented with very grotesque countenances. The knights are horses' heads and

necks, with flowing manes: the pawns, as
well as the pieces, are all different, being
eight Negroes and eight whites, of various
ages. They are as highly finished as any of
his paintings, and are in the possession of
his grandson, Mr. Gevers.

The Icelanders, who are great players,
make their men of fish bones. They have
the bishops as we have; their rooks are
officers called centurions, who are represented sounding a horn.

The modern Indian pieces are sometimes made of solid ivory, five or six inches
high. The king and queen are seated on
elephants, under a canopy, and surrounded
by their guards: the bishops are camels,
with archers as their riders, and the knights
are on horseback, both surrounded with
guards likewise; the castles are elephants, with
a great gun on each side, suspended from
the saddle, or a castle on their backs filled
with warriors; the pawns are soldiers—one
is a serjeant, another a drummer, and another a fifer, the rest private soldiers. They
are sometimes made with red and white car-

nelian, and are then very beautiful and valuable.

There appears to have been a game very like Chess, called the philosopher's game. The board of this game is eight squares in breadth, and sixteen in height. There are twenty-four men on a side, represented as flat pieces of wood, cut in the form of circles, triangles, and squares. The king is a square, on which is a triangle and a circle. " *The bottom or lower part of every man (except the two kings) must be marked with his adversary's colour, that when he is taken he may change his coat, and serve him unto whom he is prisoner.* The men are numbered, and are to be taken by *equality; obsidion; addition, substraction, multiplication, and division, and by arithmetical, geometrical, and musical proportion.*"

Carrera invented two new pieces, to be added to the eight original chess-men. That which he calls *campione* is placed between the king's knight and castle: its move is both that of the castle and of the knight. The other, named *centaur*, between the queen's knight and castle, has the move of the bishop, and knight united. Each of these pieces has its pawn, and, of course, the board must contain two more squares on each side, which will augment their number to eighty. This invention appears to have died with the inventor.

There was also another game, called Arch Chess, which likewise shared the fate of that of Carrera. This arch chess-board is like the Polish draught-board, with a hundred squares.—Two new pieces, and two pawns, are added on each side. The place of the first, called *centurion*, is between the king and his bishop, its move unites that of the queen and the castle for any two squares only, and that of the knight, so that there are sixteen places where it can go, besides its own, when in the centre of the board; but it cannot move into any of the eight squares which immediately environ it, The other piece, named *decurion*, is situated between the queen and her bishop; moves and takes as the bishop does, but only one square at a time. This piece, and the adverse one, of course stand on squares of different colours, which colours they can never quit. It will appear, that in this game, as well as in that by Carrera, the black king must at the beginning stand on a white square, and the queen, who must always be placed on a square of her own colour, will then be at his left.

The late Duke of Rutland invented a complicated game, which Sir Abraham Janssen, who was accounted, in his time, the best chess-player in England, was very much attached to. The board is 14 squares in breadth, and 10 in height, which makes 140 houses; 14 pieces and 14 pawns on a side: the pawns might move either one, two, or three squares, the first time.

The pieces were, the king, the queen, the two bishops, two knights, a crowned castle, uniting the move of the king and castle, and a common castle.

On the other side of the king, was a concubine, whose move was that of the castle and the knight united, two bishops, a single knight, a crowned castle, and a common one. The best players at this game, after Sir Abraham, were Stamma, Dr. Cowper, and Mr. Salvador. Philidor, in less than

two months, was able to give *a knight* to each
of these gentlemen at this game.

It may be observed, that the pawns are
here of very little use; and that by the extent of the board the knights lose much of
their value, which of course renders the
game more defective, and less interesting,
than the common one; and since the death
of Sir Abraham, in 1763, it is forgotten, or
at least disused.

Marshall Keith devised an amusement,
somewhat of the nature of Chess, with
which the King of Prussia was much delighted. It consisted of several thousand
statues, or men, that he would oppose to
each other in battle, and by their movements
shew the advantage or disadvantage of different modes of attack and defence.

Don John of Austria had a chamber in
which was a chequered pavement of black
and white marble: upon this, living men
moved under his direction, according to the
laws of Chess.

The same thing is told of the Duke of
Weimar, who in squares of white and black
marble played at Chess with real soldiers.

Rabelais mentions three games at Chess, played with living men and women: "*trentie deux personnaiges du bal combattent.*"

There is a curious game, in which a king and eight pawns, beat a whole set of pieces and pawns, by being allowed to make two moves to every single one of the adversary. The king with the pawns only is almost certain of winning the game, for he may make his first move into check, and his second out of it, so that he can take the queen when she stands immediately before her king, and then retreat; but he may not remain in check, neither can he himself he checkmated, unless his adversary has preserved his queen and both his castles.

In the year 1783, M. De Kempelen, an Hungarian, appeared in London with an Automaton Chess-player, which he exhibited at five shillings. This figure is as large as life, in a Turkish dress, sitting behind a table with doors, of three feet and a half in length, two in depth, and two and a half in height. The chair on which it sits is fixed to the table, which runs on four wheels: the automaton leans its right arm on the table, and in its left hand holds a pipe; with this hand it plays, after the pipe is removed. A chess-board of eighteen inches is fixed before it. This table, or rather cupboard, contains wheels, levers, cylinders, and other pieces of mechanism; all which are publicly displayed; the vestments of the automaton are then lifted over its head, and the body is seen full of similar wheels and levers: there is a little door in its thigh, which is likewise opened: and with this, and the table also open, and the automaton uncovered, the whole is wheeled about the room: the doors are then shut, and the automaton is ready to play, and it always takes the first move. At every motion the wheels are heard, the image moves its head, and looks over every part of the chess-board; when it checks the queen it shakes its head twice, and thrice in giving check to the king. It likewise shakes its head when a false move is made, replaces the piece, and makes its own move, by which means the adversary loses one.

M. De Kempelen remarked to Mr. Twiss, that though this figure had been exhibited to mathematicians and chess-players, in great part of Europe, yet the secret by which he governed the motion of the arm had never been discovered. He prided himself solely on the construction of the mechanical powers by which the arm could perform ten or twelve moves; it then required to be wound up like a watch; after which it was capable of continuing the same number of motions.

The automaton could not play unless M. De Kempelen, or his substitute, was near it to direct its moves. A small square box, during the game, was frequently consulted by the exhibitor: and herein consisted the secret, which he told Mr. Twiss he could in a moment communicate. He who could beat M. De Kempelen, was, of course, certain of conquering the automaton.

The strongest and best armed load-stone was allowed to be placed on the machine by any of the spectators.

The Monthly Review for April 1784 says, that this automaton had beaten, amongst other great players, the celebrated Mr. Philidor. But this Mr. Twiss declares to be a mistake; for that Mr. Philidor could give M. De Kempelen *a castle* and beat him.

It was the opinion of many that the whole was carried on by the help of a confederate, and a pamphlet was even published on the subject; but the minutest investigation has left no room for this suspicion.

Not altogether unconnected with the contents of this chapter is the account of a trick that may be played, of covering the sixty-four squares of the chess-board by the knight at as many moves. There are several ways of doing it; but the celebrated De Moivre having given one, which is nearly on a regular defined plan, it is presumed the reader will not be displeased at seeing it.

Supposing the squares to be numbered, beginning at the farthest left hand corner, the moves would be as follows :

The knight's first place would be on No. 8, second on 23, third on 40, fourth on 55, fifth on 61, sixth on 51, seventh on 57, eighth on 42, ninth on 25, tenth on 10, eleventh on 4, twelfth on 14, thirteenth on 24, fourteenth on 39, fifteenth on 56, sixteenth on 62, seventeenth on 52, eighteenth on 58, nineteenth on 41, twentieth on 26, twenty-first on 9, twenty-second on 3, twenty-third on 13, twenty-fourth on 7, twenty-fifth on 22, twenty-sixth on 32, twenty-seventh on 47, twenty-eighth on 64, twenty-ninth on 54, thirtieth on 60, thirty-first on 50, thirty-second on 33, thirty-third on 18, thirty-fourth on 1, thirty-fifth on 11, thirty-sixth on 5, thirty-seventh on 15, thirty-eighth on 21, thirty-ninth on 6, fortieth on 16, forty-first on 31, forty-second on 48, forty-third on 63, forty-fourth on 53, forty-fifth on 59, forty-sixth on 49, forty-seventh on 34, forty-eighth on 17, forty-ninth on 2, fiftieth on 12, fifty-first on 27, fifty-second on 44, fifty-third on 38, fifty-fourth on 28, fifty-fifth on 43, fifty-sixth on 37, fifty-seventh on 20, fifty-eighth on 35, fifty-ninth on 45, sixtieth on 30, sixty-first on 36, sixty-second on 19, sixty-third on 29, sixty-fourth on 46.

There is another trick, which will amuse the young player much more, called " Philidor s Legacy :" whether it were written by that master or not, it is clever, and deserves notice ; and the learner will find it inserted among the games.

CHAP. IV.

OF CHESS-PLAYERS, AND PUBLICATIONS ON CHESS.

———

THE following sovereigns were admirers of the game, and some of them great players.

The Emperor Charlemagne.

The Emperor Alexius Comnenus.

Richard Cœur de Lion.

Tamerlane.

Sebastian, King of Portugal.

Philip II. King of Spain.

The Emperor Charles V.

Catherine of Medicis, Queen of France.

Pope Leo X.

Henry IV. of France.

Queen Elizabeth.

Lewis XIII.

James I. King of England.

Lewis XIV.

William III.

Charles XII. King of Sweden.

Frederic, the late King of Prussia, &c.

The Prince De Tingry, a lieutenant-general in the French army, and knight of the Holy Ghost, died while playing at Chess.

The playing blind-folded, or with two or more antagonists at once, is not a novel thing. In the year 1266, there was at Florence a Saracen, named Buzecca, who played at one time at three chess-boards, with the best masters of Chess in Florence, playing with two by memory, and with the third by sight ; two games he won, and the third he made a drawn game (by a perpetual check), which circumstance was at that time esteemed marvellous.

Salvio used to play blind-folded, as appears by his book.

Keysler, in his account of Turin, in 1749, says, " The late Father Sacchieri, of Turin, was a remarkable instance of the strength of human understanding, particularly that faculty which we term memory. He could play at Chess with three different persons at the same time, even without seeing any one of the chess-boards. He required no more than that his substitute should tell him what piece his antagonist had moved, and Sacchieri could direct what step was to be taken on his side, holding at the same time conversation with the company. If any dispute arose about the place where any piece should be, he could tell every move that had been made, not only by himself but by his antagonist, from the beginning of the game; and in this manner incontestably decide the proper place of the piece."

Verci says he played to perfection on *four* chess-boards.

Sokeiker, an Arabian author, speaks of several Arabians who played at Chess blindfold, and of others who played at two boards at the same time. In the year 970, a Greek, named Jusuph Tchelebi, who had travelled through India and Persia, and seen many kingdoms, played at Chess at Tripoli, in Syria, blindfold. The chess-men which he used were very large, and he played, not by naming the moves, but by feeling the men, and placing them in the squares, or taking them off, as occasion required.

The Indians are very expert at Chess, and

it rarely happens that an European can contend with them.

The celebrated Philidor, who studied
Chess when very young under M. De Legalle, the best player in France, soon equalled,
and at length beat his master, and to the day
of his death remained unrivalled.

He was first induced to turn his mind to
the playing without seeing the board by M.
De Legalle asking him whether he had made
the attempt? to which he replied, that as
he had calculated moves, and even whole
games, in bed, he thought he could do it,
and immediately played a game with the
Abbé Chenard, which he won without seeing the board, and without hesitating upon
any of the moves.

Finding he could readily play a single
game, he offered to play two games at the
same time, which he did at a coffee-house;
and of this party, the following account is
given in the French *Encyclopédie :*

" We had at Paris a young man of eighteen,
who played at the same time two games at
Chess without seeing the boards, beating
two antagonists, to either of whom he,

though a first-rate player, could otherwise only give the advantage of *a knight*. We shall add to this account a circumstance, of which we were eye-witnesses: In the middle of one of his games a false move was designedly made, which, after a great number of moves he discovered, and placed the piece where it ought to have been at first.

On the 8th of May, 1783, he played three games at once without seeing either of the tables. His opponents were, Count Bruhl, Mr. Bowdler (the two best players in London), and Mr. Maseres. He beat the Count in an hour and twenty minutes, and Mr. Maseres, to whom he gave the king's bishop's pawn, as well as the move, which he allowed to the others, in two hours; Mr. Bowdler reduced his game to a drawn battle in an hour and three quarters.

The 10th of May, 1788, he played three games with Count Bruhl, Mr. Nowell, and Mr. Leycester, and beat each of them: to the former he gave the move, and to the latter two the king's bishop's pawn and the move.

The 13th of March, 1790, he played three

games more, with the Honourable H. S.
Conway, Captain Smith, and Mr. Sheldon,
beating them, though giving the move to
each. With Mr. Conway he saw the board.
He went through the whole with astonishing accuracy, and often corrected mistakes
in those who had the board before them.
Philidor sat with his back to the tables, and
some gentleman present, who took his part,
informed him of the moves of his antagonist
(unless he himself called them), and then by
his direction, played his pieces as he dictated.

The idea of the intellectual labour that
he was suffering at first suggested painful
sensations to the spectators, which, however,
were soon dissipated, as he seldom paused
above half a minute, and seemed to undergo
little mental fatigue, being somewhat jocose
through the whole, and uttering occasionally
many pleasantries that diverted the company.

When the intrinsic difficulty of the game
is considered, as well as the great skill of his
adversaries, he not having inexperienced,
but some of the best players in Europe to
contend with, who of course conducted it

with the most subtle complications, this exertion seems nearly miraculous, and deserves, to be recorded as a proof, at once interesting and astonishing, of the power of human intelligence.

In 1751, Philidor went to Berlin, under the hopes of playing with the King; who, however, declined it. The King saw him play several times at Potsdam, but did not play with him himself: there was a Marquis De Varennes, and a certain Jew, who played *even* with the King, and to each of these Philidor gave *a knight*, and beat them.

The best chess-players who were living in England, during the last century, were Mr. Cunningham, Lord Sunderland, Lord Godolphin, Lord Elibank, Count Bruhl, the Honourable Henry Conway, Lord Harrowby, Mr. Bowdler, Mr. Jennings, Mr. Cargyll, Sir Abraham Janssen, P. Stamma, Dr. Black, Dr. Cowper, and Mr. Salvador, and Mr. Jones.

In 1740, Philidor played a match of ten games with Stamma, giving him the move, allowing a drawn game to be a lost one, and betting five to four on each game. With

(Mr Jones bette Philidor twice.)

all these advantages, Stamma won only two games, of which one was a drawn game.

In 1770, a Chess-club was formed at the Salopian Coffee-house, Charing-cross ; and in 1774, a new one next door to the Thatched-house, in St. James Street, where it is still continued.

In 1783, a chess-club was established at Paris, in the new buildings of the Duke of Orleans, near the Palais Royal, under the protection of Monsieur, the King's brother, who was himself a member of it.

The first book on Chess was, as has been before noticed, written by Jacobus De Cœsollis, in or about the year 1200. Verci says, that the original work was written either in Latin or in French ; that the Latin manuscript is still preserved in the library of the seminary in Padua ; and that the first Italian edition was printed at Florence, in 1493, in quarto, and the second at Venice, in 1534, in octavo.

The next was a translation of the above, printed by Caxton, in 1474. This translation was made from a French one by Jehan

De Vignay, a Monk Hospitalar, and is a small folio of 144 pages.

The only book on Chess of any age in the Spanish language was printed in 1561, and is a quarto of 300 pages; the author Ruy Lopez De Sigura.

In 1617, Carrera published a quarto of 600 pages; containing an historical account of Chess and chess-players; a description of the pieces, and a number of games. In this book he gives some anecdotes of the celebrated player Paolo Boi.

Salvio published his *Il Puttino*, containing an historical account of Chess and players, with upwards of sixty games, in 1634.

Giachino Greco, known by the name of the *Calabrois*, or the *Calabrian*, published a book on Chess, which was translated into French, and printed at Paris in 1774. An English translation of it was published in London, in 24mo. in 1750.

Philip Stamma, a native of Aleppo, and interpreter of the Oriental languages at the English Court, published *The Noble Game of Chess* at London, in 1745. He seems to have been the first who specified the games by letters and figures. It appeared in French in 1737, at Paris.

Philidor published his " *Analyse du Jeu des Echecs, 12mo.* in London, in 1749; again in an octavo of 300 pages, in 1777, one in French and another in English : and again one handsomely printed, in 2 vols. in 1790. He first gave notes, explaining the nature of the moves ; which rendered his books more valuable than any that preceded ; and his method has been copied in every succeeding publication. Indeed it seems to have been thought, that a book on Chess must necessarily be connected with the name of PHILIDOR ; and accordingly we find his *Analysis* generally added, and the whole publication bearing his name.

In 1763, a most formidable Chess book was published at Bologna, called *Osservazioni Teorico-pratiche sopra il giuoco degli Scacchi. Da Giambatista Lolli, Modonese.* It is a folio of 623 pages, containing games and endings.

The Latin poem on Chess by Marcus Hieronymus Vida, Bishop of Alba, was written in 1540. It has been frequently translated into French, Spanish, Italian, and English; and the late Sir William Jones founded his elegant poem *Caïssa* on it.

In 1787 was published, " *Chess;*" a work professing to collect every thing relating to the subject: and in 1789 a second volume.

There have been innumerable other publications on Chess, in most languages, but the above are the most worthy of note.

CHAP. V.

ETYMOLOGICAL DESCRIPTION OF THE
GAME, PIECES, &c. AND EXPLANATION
OF THE TERMS MADE USE OF.

CHESS.

THE game of Chess, according to Sir William Jones, has been immemorially known in Hindostan, by the name of *Chaturanga*, or the four members of an army, *viz.* elephants, horses, chariots, and foot-soldiers.

By a corruption of the pure *Shanscrit* word, it was changed by the old Persians into *Chatrang*; but the Arabs, who soon after took possession of their country, having neither the initial nor the final letter of that word in their alphabet further altered it into *Shatranj*, which found its way into modern Persia, and at length into the dialects of India, where the true derivation of the name is known only to the learned: and thus has a very significant word in the sacred language of the Brahmins been transformed, by successive ages, into *Axedrez, Scacchi, Echecs, Chess.*

Sarasin, who wrote in 1683, has a treatise expressly on the different opinions of the origin of the Latin word *Scacchi,* from which is derived the French word *Echecs* and our *Chess.*

Leunclavius supposes it to come from *Uscoches,* famous Turkish Robbers. Sirmond from the German *Scache* (theft), and that from *Calculus.* He, as well as Vossius and Salmasius, supposes Chess to be the *Ludus Latrunculorum* of the Romans; and imagines the word *Calculus* may have been used for *Latrunculus.*

Fabricius, as before remarked, derives the name from *Schatrenscha,* a Persian astronomer, whom he takes to be the inventor. Tolosanus from the Hebrew *Scach, valavit,* and *mat, mortuus;* whence our *check* and *check-mate.*

Nicod derives it from *Schecque,* or *Xeque,* a Moorish word for lord, king, or prince.

Bochart adds, that *Scachmat* signifies *the King is dead.* Scriverius follows this opinion.

THE KING.—This piece seems always to have been so called by every writer, and in every country.

THE QUEEN—is as uniformly so called by the moderns, except the Poles and Russians, who, according to Dr. Hyde, give it also the name of the *the old woman*, or *nurse*.

The French, and after them the English, during the middle ages, called it *fierce*, *fierges*, *feers*, derived from the Persian *pherz* or *phirzin*, a *minister*, *vizier*, *counsellor*, or *general*; for it is clear that the game, however since corrupted, was originally a military one. The military spirit of the Asiatic game is still preserved in the method of playing; but the warlike characters of the actors have been almost entirely converted into those composing the principal classes of a well-regulated society—such as kings, queens, knights, bishops, fools, and peasants.

Unless the similarity in sound between the words *pherz* and *vierge* (virgin), occasioned the introduction of the latter term among the Europeans, it is difficult to account for it; it is, however, probable, that the mere sound of the word might have given rise to the whole change of the game; for the extravagant veneration of the times towards the Holy Virgin, would naturally lead to the introduction of a queen, and the rest followed of course. In an ancient Latin poem, the queen is called *virgo*.

Monsieur Freret says, " Men were soon persuaded that 'the picture of human life would be very imperfect without a woman: that sex playing too important a part not to have a place in the game, accordingly the minister was changed into *ferz*, or queen. The similarity of the words *fierge* and *vierge* facilitated the change; which appeared to be the more reasonable, as the piece is placed by the side of the king, and in the beginning could not move above two squares from him." He observes, that the romantic spirit of the times disdained this contracted motion, as rather resembling the slavery of the Asiatic females, than the privileges enjoyed by those of Europe, on which account it was rendered as free as possible, by being made it the most important of all the pieces.

. Although the title of *queen* cannot be·

traced so far back as,that of *fierce*, it is of considerable antiquity, as it is to be met with in the French MSS. and stories of the 13th century : it is there called *regina*.

M. Freret believes it is not possible to trace the term *fers*, in the English language, beyond the time of Chaucer.

In the reign of Henry VII. and indeed long before this time, the piece was called *queen*.

This change in the title of the piece occasioned an absurdity which still exists. When a pawn, or common soldier, has penetrated the enemy's battalions as far as the last line of the board, he is not allowed to return back, but is honoured with the step and prerogatives of the queen. If the *ferzin* or the *fierge* be a vizir, a first minister, or a general of an army, it is not unnatural that a common soldier should be elevated to their rank, in recompense of the valour with which he has pierced through the enemy. But if the *fierge* be a lady, a queen, or the king's wife, it is absurd to make the pawn change his sex, and become a woman.

This may be reconciled by considering,

that the incongruity obtains equally with respect to some of the other pieces. It may not be the very height of absurdity to make a soldier a bishop, but it is impossible to make him an elephant or a castle.

Jean De Vignay, in his *Moralité des Nobles Hommes*, translated from Cesolis before 1330, says, " The queen only goes from point to point, like the pawn, it not being suitable for woman to go into battle, because of her fragility and feebleness ;" so that, at that time, the queen's powers were very inconsiderable.

THE BISHOP.—The third piece at Chess, to which the English give this name, was, by our old writers called *alphyn*, *awfyn*, and *alfin;* and by the old French romancers, *aufin*, and sometimes *fol*. Hyde says, that the Spaniards, who borrowed many words from the Moors, formed the word *alfil* from the Arabic *fil* or *phil*, the name of this piece on the eastern chess-board, which signifies an *elephant*.

Rabelais calls it the *archer;* the Danes and Portuguese term it, with us, the *bishop ;*

the Germans, *lauffer*, the hound or runner;
the Spaniards and Italians, *alfil*, *alfiere*, the
standard bearer; and the Russians and
Swedes, the *elephant*.

There is no end to conjecture on the
subject of this word, which presents itself
under the successive forms of *fil*, *alfil*, *alfin*,
elphinos, (Gr.), *delphinos*, *elephas*, &c.

What was the original shape of this piece
it is also difficult to judge: Damiano, whose
book on Chess was printed in 1524, calls it
delfino, *alfil*, and *alfino*; and gives a cut of
it, as does likewise the Italian translator of
Ruy Lopez in 1584. In both their representations it resembles an urn. The French,
at a very early period, called this piece *fol*
(fool). It is natural to derive the word
as a Chess term from the original *fil*; for
it is unreasonable to suppose, that that nation, till lately, so devoted to ecclesiastical
establishments, would have introduced the
word as a satire on the clergy, however some
few of their writers might be disposed.

From this it is probable, that the ancient
term was retained after the change in the
form took place. But even if otherwise, to

account for the change is no difficult matter, when it is considered what a favourite
personage the fool was in those times. Kings
and Queens seldom appeared without their
fools. Regnier sarcastically says,—

Les foux sont aux Echecs les plus proches des rois.
                                    Sat. xiv.

A further proof that the figure of a fool
constituted one of the pieces on the ancient
French chess-board, occurs in a curious spi-
ritual romance, intitled *Le Pélerin de la vie
Humaine*, composed in the beginning of the
14th century. In this book the author has
described the chess-king, at the head of his
pieces, attacking and undermining the foun-
dations of a church. In an edition of the
translation, printed in 1504, there is a cut of
a chess-board, with a fool among the pieces.
The French yet retain this name.

It is uncertain when this piece was first
called an *archer*, or for what reason. Rabelais, in his allegorical description of the
game, has so termed it; and Colonna, the
author of *Poliphilo*, whom Rabelais copied,
has called it the *secretary*. *Archers* were

formerly the body-guards of monarchs, and
might have been thought by some more
proper in the game of Chess than *fools*, especially if they were inclined to give it a military turn. Vida, in his poem on Chess,
describes this piece as an *archer;* and Beale,
who published a translation of *Biochimos's
Royal Game of Chesse-play*, in 1656, makes
the *bishop* and *archer* the same, with a cloven
head.

It is, perhaps, impossible to trace the first
appearance of this piece with a forked or
broken head. It is represented something
in this manner in Caxton's translation of
Jacobus De Cessolis; but his *rook* is given
as still more so. The English and Danes
alone, in modern times, call it the *bishop;*
and the first mention of this term in England is in *Saul's famous Game of Chesse-play*,
originally published in 1640, who says,
" The game resembles a well-composed
commonwealth; the bishops representing
the clergy, with high cloven heads, like a
bishop's mitre."

The word *cornua* was used in the middle
ages for a mitre; but whether the *cornu*

formed a separate piece in the ancient European game, or whether the term was synonymous with the *alfin*, is not quite clear. There is, however, great reason to think that the *alfin*, the *cornu*, and the *bishop*, were in fact the same.

In a very old Latin poem upon Chess, printed by Dr. Hyde, *De Ludis Orient.* p. 179, from a MS. in the Bodleian Library, the piece next the king is termed *calvus;* and, if this denotes a monk with a shaven crown, it is another very early instance of the introduction of *priests* among the chess-men.

THE KNIGHT has been always so called upon the European chess-boards. It is probable that he was represented, in the earliest times, as *mounted on his charger :* Vida has so described him ; and the natives of India, as before remarked, frequently make him so in their large sets. Hence, in modern times it has been termed the *horse*, and so represented. The Spaniards and Italians have adopted both these names, but give it the form of a *horse's head :* which is the figure generally used by us.

THE ROOK.—The origin of our *rook* may be found in the old French term *roc,* or, as it is sometimes mentioned in old MS. poems, *ros* ; not that this French word de-noted, upon this occasion, *rock* or *fortress,* but that it was immediately borrowed, toge-ther with the Spanish and Italian terms, from *ruc,* the eastern name of this piece. It is, indeed, difficult to say, what .the original *form* of it was on the European chess-board: the oldest we know of is that represented in Caxton's translation of Jacobus De Cessolis, and which is like a mitre with the points in-clining outwards, or like two elephant's tusks diverging from each other. It is likewise to be found, under the same .shape, in books of heraldry, under the name of *chess-rook.*

Dr. Hyde thinks, that its forked head is expressive of the two bunches upon the back of the *dromedary,* under which figure it occurs upon the eastern chess-boards; and he has given representations of the Turkish chess-men, in which this piece exactly re-sembles that of Caxton.

M. D'Herbelot informs us, that *rokh,* in the Persian language, signifies a *valiant hero seeking after military adventures*, in which character, he says, it was introduced into the game of Chess.

Sir William Jones says, that the *rook* is to be deduced from the *rat'h* of the old Hindoo game of Chess, which was an *armed chariot*. This the Persians changed into *rokh*; of which word, he adds, the etymology has in vain been sought for.

The term *castle* and the French word *tour* may have arisen from confounding the old French word *roc* with *rocca*, a fortress; or the European form of the castle may have been copied in part from the *elephant and castle* on his back. It is thus described by Vida; and whilst the English, French, Spaniards, and Italians have retained the *castle* only, the Danes, Germans, and Indians have adopted the *elephant* without the castle; by the former of which names it is also called by them. By the Poles this piece is also termed the *rook*; the Russians make it a *boat*, or rather its *keel*: Dr. Hyde supposes this to be from its length, or the velocity of its motion; which, he says, in the eastern chess-board, originated from the manner in which the dromedary travels. The Swedes, according to the same author, call it the *leaper*, and have made it change places with the *bishop*. Among Charlemagne's pieces, it is termed the *elephant*.

THE PAWNS.—These appear to have been always so called among ourselves; and by the French, in the middle ages, *paon*, *paon-net*, *paonnez*, *paonniers*, *poons*, *poonnes*, and *pionnes*. In the Romance of the Rose they are called *garçons*. They are all, probably, from *pedones*, a barbarous Latin term for *foot-soldiers*; which, in this game, were re-presented by the pawns. By the Italians they are now called *pedone*, by the Spaniards *peones*. The Russians and Poles make them also *foot-soldiers*. The Germans, Danes, and Swedes have converted them into *pea-sants*.

The writers of the middle ages, in speaking of the chess-men, universally style them *familia* or *familiæ*.

CASTLING.—Is the moving the king two squares, leaping over one, either on his own side or on that of his queen, and placing the castle on the square over which he leaped.

The old way of castling, and which is still used in some countries, was to leave it to the player's option to place his king on any one of the squares of the last row, those of the rooks included. The mode now mentioned is that which is adopted by Philidor. The king can castle but once in the game; and not then even, in case of his either being actually *in check*, or *having before moved*, or *being exposed to check in passing over any square* commanded by an adversary, or with a rook that has been *previously moved*, or if there is any piece *between* him and the rook.

The *propriety* of this arrangement, and of some of these limitations, is strongly called in question, by a late publication, on the grounds, first, that the arrangement is destructive of uniformity; since the king, after having castled, will, if on his own rook's side, stand one square from the end; while on his queen's side he will be two squares: and the writer conceives, that as in the latter case the rook will have to leap over two squares instead of one, as, on the king's side, the advantage of leaping the additional square might, with more propriety, be given to the king than the rook: and, secondly, that the prohibition from castling, when he is in danger, is as extraordinary as if a general, pressed on all sides, were prevented taking refuge under the guns of a fort.; that very interesting situations occur by allowing the king to castle when in check, which cannot under a contrary precaution; and that the prohibiting his passing a square commanded by an adversary is absurd, because not general with respect to the other pieces; and if it were general, " Chess would have a constitution most ingeniously impracticable."

Though I have thus inserted these opinions, the remark I shall content myself with making on the subject is, that in all laws CERTAINTY is the most desirable object; and that a law had better be a little doubtful as to its justice than as to its operation. In the legislation of Chess, Philidor may be considered despotic, and his laws being implicitly adopted by the chess-clubs

in London and Paris, perhaps the inconve-
nience suffered by following them will be
much less than the difficulty would be of
making chess-players unanimous on any
proposed alteration.

In castling there is the double object, of
placing the king in a more secure place, and
bringing the rook immediately into play.

MAKING A PAWN A QUEEN, &c.—
Whenever a pawn has reached the last row
of the adversary's end of the chess-board,
he may be exchanged for any piece the
player pleases, although he has not previously lost one. This is contained in Philidor's IXth Law : but it must be noticed, it
has been a subject of much dispute and con-
tradiction, and even Philidor has contra-
dicted himself upon it. Notwithstanding
the express law, the meaning of which appears plain and unequivocal, he in a late edition of his *Analysis* has the following passage :—speaking of, and freely blaming the
innovations introduced into play by the
Germans, he says, " While this field of cri-
ticism lies open, I cannot pass by my own

countrymen, who have committed as great
a fault as the Germans. They are less to
be excused, there being many good players
among them, nay, some of them the best in
Europe. I presume they have been led
away (like myself formerly) by a bad custom,
established, in all probability, by the persons who first brought Chess into France;
I am inclined to think it must have been
some player at draughts, who knowing little more than the moves of the pieces, ima-
gined one might make as many queens in
the game at Chess as at draughts. I would
only ask, what a fine sight it is to see upon
the chess-board, two pawns on the same
square, to distinguish a second queen; and
if by chance a third should be made (as I
have often seen at Paris), then it is still a
finer sight, while the bottom of the pawn is
almost sufficient to cover a square on the
board! Is not, therefore, this method most
ridiculous, especially as it is practised in
no country where the game of Chess is
known? However, if my countrymen will
go on in this erroneous way, I would advise
them, to prevent all disputes that may arise

about their multiplicity of queens, to make to each set of chess-men three or four queens, as many rooks, knights, &c."

The writer above-mentioned forms a candid supposition, that perhaps Philidor, in yielding to the mode, contained in the 1Xth Law, was overborn by a majority, prepossessed in favour of a practice to which from their first acquaintance with the game they had been accustomed. A great difficulty still overpowers the question : I have now before me an edition containing the laws published in 1790, and the one from which the above extract from Philidor is cited was printed in 1791 ; both before Philidor's death, which took place in 1795.

The Indians, when their pawn has attained the line of the adversary's pieces, if it steps into the queen's, bishop's, knight's, or rook's houses, make it that officer whose station he has taken, provided such a one has previously been lost; otherwise the pawn must be endeavoured to be protected till the requisite vacancy happens.

CHECK.—As on the political board *the*

king never dies, so on the chess-board *the king is never taken ;* and, therefore, when‑ ever he is attacked, and in such a situation as were he an inferior piece he would be cap‑ tured, notice is immediately given him of his danger by the word *check.*

DOUBLE CHECK—is when it is given by two pieces at once, and which is not uncommon; for example—a bishop may stand before a rook, so that neither gives check, when by moving, and checking with the bishop, the rook may give check by discovery also ; and the same with the other pieces. There are three ways of getting out of *check; first,* by taking the piece attacking him, either by himself or one of his party : and this can only be done, in the case of double check, if one of the pieces does not guard the other. *Secondly,* by interposing a piece between him and the threatener ; which also cannot be done in the case of double check, or against a knight. *Thirdly,* by removing to another square which no hostile piece commands.

CHECKMATE—is when neither of these is in his power; he is therefore *checkmated*, and the game is at an end.

It is almost needless to say, that one king cannot give check to the other, since, by it, he himself stands in a similar situation.

There are different ways of giving *check-mate*, as follow :—

CHECKMATE *by Discovery*—which is when an adverse piece is opposed to the king, but is for the time incapable of injury, owing to a piece standing between him and the king: the discovery takes place when this latter piece is removed, and in case the piece removed is a hostile one; so that the discovered check arises by the act of the enemy. It is considered a master-stroke, and frequently fatal.

BLIND MATE—is that which is given unwittingly, and not perceived till it has been done; which, of course, is productive of but little merit, and in France, when the game is played strictly, only half the stake (if there be any) is won.

SMOTHERED MATE—is when the king is so surrounded by his own friends that he cannot move out of check for them; and this mate is generally given by the knight.

FORCED MATE — is that which is clearly seen to be inevitable, though a few desperate sacrifices might for a while protract it.

STALE MATE—called *le pat* by the French, and *lo stallo* by the Italians, from *stall*, a dwelling place, because the king remains in his place,—is when the king, *not being in check*, is so crowded up either by his own or his adversary's pieces that he cannot move *without going into check*, and at the same time has no other piece to move. In this case, he is allowed with us to win the game; in France, however, it is made a drawn game.

DRAWN GAME.—This must frequently happen between equal players; and most commonly is occasioned by one of the five following means : *First*, by a perpetual check ; *secondly*, by the two king's remaining alone on the field of battle ; *thirdly*, by each king having only a single piece at the end of the game, without any local advantage on either side ; *fourthly*, by the game being so situated, that both sides are on the defensive, and neither will be the first to yield and lose the advantage of his situation ; and *lastly*, when the king, having lost all his men, is not *mated* in fifty moves, from the unskilfulness of his enemy, according to Law XVII.

LA TAVOLA—means that kind of drawn game which is occasioned by continual checks. The French term it, *L'echec perpetuel*.

GAMBIT, *Il Gambetto, L'antarella, la Gambarola, Jambette, Croc en jambe.*—The real meaning of this word is doubtful ; it appears to be an expression borrowed from wrestling, when a man throws his adversary by a particular stroke of the leg. At Chess it means that kind of game which begins with pushing the king's and king's bishop's pawn two squares each, instead of making one defend the other; or the queen's and queen's bishop's pawn. The pawn first pushed is called the gambit-pawn: this game is founded rather on experiment than on system. The surrender of the pawn, indeed, is a common feature in all the gambits; but afterwards the moves vary so much, and depend so greatly on the spirit of the player, that little connexion can be discovered. It appears, however, that a gambit, equally well played on both sides, will be indecisive; though the power, which he who sacrifices the pawn has, of always attacking, will be fatal, unless the other party play uniformly well the first ten or twelve moves.

It must be remarked, too, that playing the gambit is in no wise advantageous when a piece is given to the adversary.

EN PRISE.—A piece is said to be *en prise*, when it is in the adversary's power to capture it.

CHAP. VI.

FRANKLIN'S MORALS OF CHESS.

———

THE following little treatise on Chess might with great propriety have accompanied the anecdotes, expressive of the violent effects the game has had on the mind and passions. It will not, however, unaptly precede the practical rules and directions, since the precepts laid down are so admirably calculated to allay, as well the transports of victory, as the chagrin of defeat, that it will not be amiss to consider them as forming an essential part of the rules.

This treatise was the production of Dr. Franklin; whose comprehensive mind, like the proboscis of an elephant, was alike capable of wielding the most mighty, and grasping the most minute subject.

"Playing at Chess is the most ancient and most universal game among men; for its original is beyond the memory of history, and it has, for numberless ages, been the amusement of all the civilized nations of Asia, the Persians, the Indians, and the Chinese. Europe has had it above a thousand years; the Spaniards have spread it over their part of America, and it begins lately to make its appearance in these States. It is so interesting in itself, as not to need the view of gain to induce engaging in it; and thence it is never played for money. Those, therefore, who have leisure for such diversions, cannot find one that is more innocent; and the following piece, written with a view to correct (among a few young friends) some little improprieties in the practice of it, shews, at the same time, that it may, in its effects on the mind, be not merely innocent, but advantage-ous, to the vanquished as well as the victor.

" The game of Chess is not merely an idle amusement. Several very valuable qualities of the mind, useful in the course of human life, are to be acquired or strengthened by it, so as to become habits, ready on all occasions. For life is a kind of Chess, in which we have often points to gain, and competitors or adversaries to contend with, and in which there is a vast variety of good and ill events, that are, in some degree, the effects of prudence or the want of it. By playing at Chess, then, we learn,

"I. *Foresight*, which looks a little into futurity, and considers the consequences that may attend an action : for it is continually occurring to the player, ' If I move this piece, what will be the advantage of my new situation? What use can my adversary make of it to annoy me? What other moves can I make to support it, and defend myself from his attacks?'

"II. *Circumspection*, which surveys the whole chess-board, or scene of action; the relation of the several pieces, and their situations; the dangers they are repeatedly exposed to; the several possibilities of their aiding each other; the probabilities that the adversary may make this or that move, and attack this or that piece; and what different means can be used to avoid his stroke, or turn its consequences against him.

"III. *Caution*, not to make our moves too

hastily. This habit is best acquired by observing strictly the laws of the game; such as, ' If you touch a piece, you must move it somewhere; if you set it down, you must let it remain.'

" Therefore, it would be the better way to observe these rules, as the game becomes thereby more the image of human life, and particularly of war; in which, if you have incautiously put yourself into a bad and dangerous position, you cannot obtain your enemy's leave to withdraw your troops, and place them more securely, but you must abide all the consequences of your rashness.

" And lastly, we learn by Chess the habit of not being discouraged by present bad appearances in the state of our affairs; the habit of hoping for a favourable change, and that of persevering in the search of resources. The game is so full of events, there is such a variety of turns in it, the fortune of it is so subject to sudden vicissitudes, and one so frequently, after contemplation, discovers the means of extricating oneself from a supposed insurmountable difficulty, that one is encouraged to con-

time the contest to the last, in hopes of victory from our skill, or, at least, from the negligence of our adversary. And whoever considers, what in Chess he often sees instances of, that success is apt to produce presumption, and its consequent, inattention, by which more is afterwards lost than was gained by the preceding advantage, while misfortunes produce more care and attention, by which the loss may be recovered, will learn not to be too much discouraged by any present successes of his adversary, nor to despair of final good fortune, upon every little check he receives in the pursuit of it.

"That we may therefore be induced more frequently to chuse this beneficial amusement, in preference to others which are not attended with the same advantages, every circumstance that may increase the pleasure of it should be regarded: and every action or word that is unfair, disrespectful, or that in any way may give uneasiness, should be avoided, as contrary to the immediate intention of both the parties, which is to pass the time agreeably:

" I. Therefore, if it is agreed to play according to the strict rules, then those rules are to be strictly observed by both parties; and should not be insisted upon for one side, while deviated from by the other, for this is not equitable.

",II. If it is agreed not to observe the rules exactly, but one party demands indulgences, he should then be as willing to allow them to the other.

" III. No false move should ever be made to extricate yourself out of a difficulty or to gain an advantage; for there can be no pleasure in playing with a man once detected in such unfair practice.

. " IV. If your adversary is long in playing, you ought not to hurry him, or express any uneasiness at his delay; not even by looking at your watch, or taking up a book to read: you should not sing, nor whistle, nor make a tapping with your feet on the floor, or with your fingers on the table, nor do any thing that may distract his attention; for all these things displease, and they do not prove your skill in playing, but your craftiness, and your rudeness.

" V. You ought not to endeavour to amuse
and deceive your adversary, by pretending
to have made bad moves: and saying you
have now lost the game, in order to make
him secure and careless, and inattentive to
your schemes; for this is fraud and deceit,
not skill in the game of Chess.

" VI. You must not, when you have gained
a victory, use any triumphing or insulting
expressions, nor shew too much of the
pleasure you feel; but endeavour to con-
sole your adversary, and make him less
dissatisfied with himself by every kind and
civil expression that might be used with
truth; such as, you understand the game
better than I, but you are a little inattentive,
or you play too fast; or you had the best
of the game, but something happened to
divert your thoughts, and that turned it
in my favour.

" VII. If you are a spectator, while
others play, observe the most perfect si-
lence; for if you give advice, you offend
both parties; him against whom you give
it, because it may cause him to lose the
game; him in whose favour you give it,

because, though it be good, and he follows
it, he loses the pleasure he might have had,
if you had permitted him to think till it occurred to himself. Even, after a move, or
moves, you must not, by replacing the
pieces, show how they might have been
placed better; for that displeases, and might
occasion disputes, or doubts about their
true situation.

" All talking to the players, lessens or di-
verts their attention, and is, therefore, un-
pleasing; nor should you give the least
hint to either party by any kind of noise or
motion, if you do, you are unworthy of
being a spectator. •

" If you desire to exercise or shew your
judgment, do it in playing your own game,
when you have an opportunity, not in cri-
ticising or meddling with, or counselling the
play of others.

" Lastly, If the game is not to be played
rigorously, according to the rules above
mentioned, then moderate your desire of
victory over your adversary, and be pleased
with one over yourself.

" Snatch not eagerly at every advantage

offered by his unskilfulness or inattention; but point out to him kindly, that by such a move, he places or leaves a piece *en prise* unsupported; that by another, he will put his king into a dangerous situation, &c.

" By this generous civility (so opposite to the unfairness above forbidden) you may happen indeed to lose the game, but you will win what is better, his esteem, his respect, and his affection; together with the silent approbation and the good-will of the spectators."

To this may be added the following, though by another pen, since it so well accords with the spirit of what precedes:

" When a vanquished player is guilty of an untruth to cover his disgrace, as ' I have not played so long; his method of opening the game confused me;—the men were of an unusual size,' &c. All such apologies (to call them no worse) must lower him in a wise person's eyes, both as a man, and as a chess-player; and who will not suspect that he, who shelters himself under such untruths in trifling matters, is no very sturdy moralist in things of greater conse-

quences, where his fame or honour are at
stake? A man of proper pride would scorn
to account for his being beaten, by one of
these excuses, even if it were true; because
they all have so much the appearance, at
the moment, of being untrue."

PLAN OF THE CHESS BOARD.

BLACK MEN.							
Queen's Rook.	Queen's Knight. ¶	Queen's Bishop.	Queen. ¶	King.	King's Bishop. ¶	King's Knight.	King's Rook. ¶
Q. R. Pawn. ¶	Q. Kt. Pawn.	Q. B. Pawn. ¶	Queen's Pawn.	King's Pawn. ¶	K. B. Pawn.	K. Kt. Pawn. ¶	K. R. Pawn.
	¶		¶		¶		¶
¶		¶		¶		¶	
	¶		¶		¶		¶
¶		¶		¶		¶	
Q. R. Pawn.	Q. Kt. Pawn. ¶	Q. B. Pawn.	Queen's Pawn. ¶	King's Pawn.	K. B. Pawn. ¶	K. Kt. Pawn.	K. R. Pawn. ¶
Queen's Rook. ¶	Queen's Knight.	Queen's Bishop. ¶	Queen.	King. ¶	King's Bishop.	King's Knight. ¶	King's Rook.
WHITE MEN.							

This Mark ¶ represents the Black Squares.

CHAP. VI.

PRACTICAL DESCRIPTION OF THE GAME,
PIECES, AND MOVES.

———————

THE chess-board, like that used at Draughts, contains sixty-four squares, eight by eight, alternately white and black; but there ex‑ ist many differences between them. In the draught-board the white squares only are used, but at Chess both black and white are played upon; and therefore a chess-board may properly be made with brown and white squares, so great a distinction not be‑ ing wanted as in the other.

In Draughts, the right hand square is a *black* one; the men are *leaped over* in being taken, and you are compelled by the rules of the game to take any man that stands in the way; in all of which Chess differs. I am thus particular, because, most probably, many may learn Chess who have a previous knowledge of Draughts.

H

The squares are called *houses*; the lines running from left to right are called *ranks*; and those perpendicular to them, or from top to bottom, *files*. In playing, the white corner square must be. at the right hand of each player : and, it is said, the Greeks adopted this disposition, as considering that colour on the right to be an omen of victory.

The best size for a chess-board is about 18 inches, giving two inches to each square.

THE PIECES—are sixteen on each side, eight pawns and eight dignified pieces; so that they occupy half the board. These are distinguished by the colours black and white, red and white, green and white, &c. &c. The pieces are the king and queen, and two bishops, two knights, and two rooks : these are called the king's, or queen's bishops, &c. according as they stand on the one side or the other. Their positions are as follow, according to the plan page 96.

The white king is placed on the middle black square, being the fourth from the right hand corner ; his queen on the white square to the left of him ; a bishop next to each, then a knight, and lastly a rook. The black pieces are placed directly opposite ; the king opposite the king, the queen the same ; so that the queens will each stand on her own proper colour. This distribution will cause the black queen to be at the right of *her* king, though the white one is at the left of hers ; and, on this account, every player should accustom himself early to play with either colour. The pawns stand on the second row, one before each piece from which they respectively take their names. Each description of piece has its own peculiar move.

THE PAWNS—move only one square at a time, from their own end towards that of the adversary ; except at first, when each has the liberty of moving two squares, unless the square over which he leaps is commanded by a hostile pawn, so that if he were to rest on that square, instead of leaping over it, he might be captured : in such case, the adverse pawn has the option of taking him, and placing himself on the square leaped

over, (see Law X.) This liability to be
so taken does not prevail in Italy, and some
other places, and seems to cause a little dis-
satisfaction even with us. The pawn cannot recede, as all the other pieces may, but
must go forwards, till, like the men at
draughts, he attains the adversary's last row,
when he is exchanged for a queen, or other
piece, at his option. Though his regular
march is straight forwards, yet he cannot
take a pawn or piece standing directly before
him, but those that stand in the squares
diagonally before him. In this he differs
from all the other pieces, who take in the
direction in which they move. After every
capture, he continues to go forward as before. The king's bishop's pawn is considerd
the most valuable.

THE KNIGHT—moves the eighth part
of a circle; that is, from the square he
stands on to the one of a different colour
two squares distant, or next but one to him,
passing over one *side* of a square and one
corner; as from his own to the adjoining
bishop's, or rook's third square. He is

the only piece which, as his figure on our
boards exclusively indicates, can leap over
the others in his way; so that he might be
brought out, if expedient, before a pawn
is played, and no interposition of another
piece will avail against him: this renders
him particularly formidable in the beginning
of the game, as he can enter into the adversary's game, and retire, notwithstanding
almost any blockade; and if he can check
the king, without being himself liable to be
taken, the king *must* remove, and cannot
afterwards castle. There is still, however,
one corrective to this great power, he can
neither stop short of, nor pass a limited extent, like the other pieces.

The following may be worthy the learner's
attention:—A knight can check a piece on
the next square to him, *of the same colour*,
at *one* move; but of *a different colour* at
two moves: also one two squares in a line
from him (one square between), if the square
between be *a different colour*, at *one* move—
if the *same colour*, then at not less than *three*
moves: also three squares from him if they
both *stand on the same colours* at *one* move;

if they stand on *different colours*, then at
two moves.   He can check across the board,
laterally, in *four* moves—diagonally, in *five* ;
though he can go across the board to check on
an *adjoining line* in *three* moves.   He cannot
check a piece standing on a *different colour*
(not already in *check*) in less than two moves.

If he has a piece in *check* he cannot again
check it at the following move.   If he checks
a *knight*, he himself is in check to that
knight.

When in the middle of the board, he
commands a circle of eight squares, of a different colour to that on which he himself
stands ; so that he has always, if the limits
of the board will permit, and they are not
occupied by one of his own party, eight
squares to go to.

The above will be easily conceivable b y
the learner, on his considering, that the
knight's move is always *from one colour to
another ;* so that what he checks at any even
number of moves he cannot at an odd, and
so *vice versa.*

THE BISHOP—moves diagonally over

any number of squares, or from one end of
the board to the other; always in a line
and on the colour he is first placed on.
The king's bishop is accounted the better one, principally because he can check
the king on his original square, which the
queen's bishop cannot. It must be remem-
bered, that the *king's* bishops, on both sides,
move on their own colours; the white bishop
on white squares, and the black on black;
the queen's bishops of course, therefore,
vice versa; or again, *that the king's bishops
move on the colours their respective queens
are of.* This piece, like the rook and queen,
can take at any distance.

THE ROOK—moves along the *files,* or
ranks, and not diagonally as the bishop;
like him, though, he can go, or stop short
of, any length, and take at any distance.
He has a very considerable advantage over
the bishop in this, that when on a rank or
file, at the margin of the board, there is no
escape for his adversary on that side, the
border acting in some degree, if it may be
so said, as another rook. This is evidently

not the case with the bishop, whose diagonal cannot be so flanked, and must leave two sides for his adversary to escape. He is not useful early, but is particularly so at the conclusion of a game; possessing the power of giving *checkmate* with the king alone, which neither the bishop nor knight can do*.

THE QUEEN—is almost unlimited in her moves, as she unites those of the bishop and the rook, and is, therefore, the most valuable piece on the board. The Russians give, as was observed in the first Chapter, the additional move of the knight, and it would seem she must then be nearly invincible.

THE KING—can move but one square at a time (except in the case of castling, as

---

* The rook is less useful than the bishop at the outset of the game, and the reason is easily explained: the bishop, moving diagonally on *one* colour only, meets with fewer impediments: the opposite bishop and his own never stand in his way, and the pawns, supporting each other, leave the *diagonal* lines in general free;—on the contrary, the rook, moving over *each* colour, finds obstruction every where.

before described); this may be either forwards or backwards, sideways or diagonally. His walk, therefore, is more circumscribed than that of either of the other pieces, and even the exclusive privilege he has of *never being taken* cannot be considerd a benefit, since it only means, that he *cannot move into* or *continue in danger*. He is, however, after all, the head and main-spring of the game; since, when he is *checkmated*, the whole is finished, although not a piece on the board may have been lost.

The square on which a piece is placed is called its own, as the king's square, king's bishop's square, &c. the next, on which the pawn stands, is called the second square; the next two, the third and fourth. In particularizing the games, the squares, after the fourth, are called the adversary's, or black or white, according as the adversary's colour is.

OF BEGINNING THE GAME.—In the game of Chess there are two objects in view, or two modes of winning: *First*, by giving *checkmate;* which may be done, as before observed, though hardly a piece is lost: *Secondly,* by such frequent captures and exchanges that the power on one side is comparatively reduced to nothing, and the *mate* is a necessary consequence.

The right to the first move is decided by lot thus : one of the parties takes a pawn from each side, and holds in his closed hands; the other calls his pawn, and if he guesses the hand in which it is, he has the move, otherwise not. Afterwards it goes alternately.

No move can be liable to so little exception at Chess as the pushing the king's pawn two squares, for the opening the game. The reasons for this move are principally these: *First,* it leaves the queen, and king's bishop at liberty to act, without exposing the king. *Secondly,* the rooks are useless at the beginning of the game ; and therefore their pawns pushed out are not only unnecessary; but they take with them a great safe-guard which the king would find when he castles. And, *thirdly,* the knights, who are the most useful at this stage, can come into play with-

out *their* pawns being moved. *All* Philidor's games (except the *queen's* gambit,
expressly so called from the queen's pawn
moving first) begin thus ; and no affectation
of novelty should induce the learner to do
otherwise. If this pawn is threatened (which
it will rarely be in the first instance, nothing
but the king's knight being able so to do),
the queen's or bishop's pawn may support
it. The future moves are not to be defined
by theory. The *Calabrois* generally brought
out his king's knight to his king's bishop's
third square, for his second move ; but this
mode is reprobated by Philidor, as will be
seen by his third party.

GENERAL REMARKS.—The mode of
capture by any piece, or pawn, is the taking
off the captured piece, and placing himself
in his stead. Any piece may be captured
that stands on any one of the squares the
piece ranges over, except in the case of the
knight, who can only take on the third
square, and not on the one he leaps over, and
of the pawn who does not take on the square

he might have moved to, but on that lying diagonally before him on the right or left.

The power of taking is *reciprocal;* so that any adverse piece you can take, may take you. The goodness of play, therefore, consists in having the greatest number of pieces defending, so that in case of mutual exchanges you may gain more than your adversary. The power of taking is also *general;* and is inherent in the pawn as well as in the king, queen, &c. each taking every thing within its range. It is also *optional;* as the beautiful variety of the game would be lost were it otherwise, as at Draughts.

A piece guards another, when he is so placed that he might capture the one guarded were he an adversary; so that the protection arises from the fear of reprisal. The king alone must be defended by placing his guard *between* him and the danger, as he must not in any case be taken.

The arrangement of the pieces, according to their real powers, is as follows :—*Pawn, Knight, King, Bishop, Rook, Queen.* The power each may be said to possess is about

Pawn - - - - $2\frac{1}{5}$ Bishop - - - $9\frac{3}{4}$

Knight - - - $6\frac{1}{4}$ Rook - - - - 15

King - - - - $7\frac{1}{2}$ Queen - - - $23\frac{3}{4}$

The *value* of each is commensurate with the *power*, except that of the pawn and the king. If the pawn's chance of promotion be taken into the question, his value will be $4\frac{7}{8}$. And the nature of the game, making the king inviolable, *his* value is above all calculation.

The knowledge of these powers is necessary, in order to appreciate exchanges that may be offered. But, as every player's mode must differ, the learner will himself fix an imaginary value, depending on his own and his adversary's prevailing method.

CHAP. VIII.

LAWS OF CHESS,

AND ELEMENTARY RULES FOR PLAYING.

THE laws, as established under the authority of Philidor, are thus elegantly introduced by him:—" The laws, or constitutions of a game are originally established, either to prevent or decide contests; because, by defining what is in itself indefinite, by determining that which, without any explanation, would be uncertain, they put an end to all obstinacy and dispute. These statutes, founded at first in reason, consecrated afterwards by custom, confirmed at length by the practice of the best players, and the approbation of the most illustrious authors, may be reduced to the XVII following Laws; which the Society or Club of Chess in England have adopted for their code."

LAWS.

I.

The chess-board must be turned in such a manner, that both players may have the white square at their right hands.

II.

He that gives a piece is supposed to have the move, unless it be agreed otherwise. In games without odds, lots must be cast for the move; afterwards it becomes alternate.

III.

If a pawn or piece has been forgotten at the beginning of the game, it will be in the adversary's choice, either to begin the game afresh, or to go on, permitting nevertheless the piece forgotten to be again set in its place.

IV.

If it is agreed to give the advantage of a piece or a pawn, and it has been forgotten at the beginning of the game, it will be left to the choice of him who has suffered by such a mistake, to go on with the game, or to begin it again.

V.

A piece once touched must be played, unless it is said, in touching it, *j'adoube**: but if by chance it is displaced or overturned, it will be allowed to put it right, and set it again in its place.

VI.

If you touch one of your adversary's pieces without saying *j'adoube*, he has a right to oblige you to take it ; and in case it was not takeable, you, who have touched it, must play your king, if you can.

VII.

When one has quite left a piece, he cannot take it again, to play to another place ; but so long as he keeps his hold of it, he is at liberty to play it where he pleases.

VIII.

Whoever makes a false move, must play his king, as in Law VI. but no false

---

* " I replace." It is a word made use of only at *Chess*, or *Tric-trac*, when a person touching a piece intimates that he does it only to adjust, and not to play it. The word seems to have arisen from *radouber*, to refit or repair a ship.

move can be recalled after the adversary's
next move : so the position must remain,
as if such irregular move, not revoked in
time, had been just.

IX.

Every pawn which has reached the
eighth, or last square of the chess-board, is
entitled to make a queen, or any other
piece that shall be thought proper ; and this
even when all the pieces remain on the
chess-board.

X.

Any pawn has the privilege of advancing two squares, at its first move: but, in
this case, it may, in passing, be taken by any
pawn which might have taken it if it had
been pushed but one move.

XI.

The king, when he castles, cannot go
beyond two squares: that is, the rook
with which he castles must take its place
next to the king; and this last, leaping
over, will be posted on the other side of the
rook *.

---

* The old way of castling, in several countries, and
which still subsists in some, was to leave to the player's

I

XII.

The king cannot castle when in check, nor after having been moved, nor if in passing he was exposed to a check, nor with a rook which has been removed from its place... And he that castles when he should not do it, must play his rook touched, or his king, at his own choice.

XIII.

If a player gives check without warning, the adversary will not be bound to ward it off; and he may consequently play as if such check did not exist; but if the first, in playing the next move, were to say, *Check!* each must then come back from his last move, as being false, and he that is under check is to take it off.

XIV.

If the adversary warns you of a check, without, however, giving it, and you in consequence touch either your king, or any other piece, you will then be allowed to retract your move so long as your adversary has not yet made his next move.

---

disposal all the interval between the king and the rook, inclusively, to place therein these two pieces.

XV.

If any one touches a piece which he cannot play without opening check, he must then play his king; and if his king cannot be played, the fault is of no consequence.

XVI.

When one has nothing else to play, and his king being out of check cannot stir, without coming to a check, then the game is stale-mate. In England, he whose king is stale-mate wins the game*; but in France, and several other countries, the stale-mate is a drawn game.

XVII.

At all the conclusions of parties, when a player seems not to know how to give the difficult mates, as that of a knight and a bishop against the king, that of a rook and a bishop against a rook, &c. at the adversary's request, fifty moves on either side must be appointed for the end of the game: these moves being over, it will be a drawn game.

---

* This rule is grounded on the decision of several authors; particularly, it is to be found in the edition of the *Calabrois*, printed in London in the year 1656.

RULES.

(A).   ON OPENING THE GAME.

1. Move your pawns before you do your pieces, and afterwards bring out your pieces to support them; the king's, queen's, and bishop's pawns, should be the first played, in order to open your game well.

2. Play your men in so good guard of one another, that if any man you advance be taken, the adverse piece may also be taken by that which guarded yours; for this purpose have as many guards to your piece as you see your adversary advances pieces upon it, and, if you can, let them be of less value than those he assails with. If you find that you cannot well support your piece otherwise, see if by attacking one of his that is better, or as good, you can thereby save it.

3. Do not inconsiderately push on the pawns either of your king or queen's side, before your adversary's king has castled; he will otherwise retire to the side where they are less strong or less advanced.

4. Pawns, when sustained in a front line, hinder very much your adversary's pieces entering your game, or taking an advantageous post.

5. If possible, dispose your pawns in such a manner as to hinder the knight's entering into your game.

6. When you have two pawns in a front line, push neither of them before your adversary proposes to change one for one of his; then, instead of exchanging, push forwards the attacked pawn.

7. One or two pawns too far advanced in the beginning of the game, may be reckoned as lost, except when all the pieces are fit for action, or the pawns when taken can have their places supplied by other pawns.

8. Two pawns in a front line, situated upon your fourth squares, are better than two upon the sixth squares; because being so distant from the main body, the latter may be compared to a forlorn hope.

9. When two bodies of pawns are separated from the centre, endeavour to increase the strongest side: and if you have two pawns in the centre, unite as many there as possible.

10. A pawn passed, and well supported, often costs the adversary a piece; while a pawn separated from his companions, is seldom worth any thing. The knight's or rook's pawns, when separated from the centre, are of but little consequence. Two pawns, with an interval between, can be considered no better than one; and if you should have three over each other in a line, your game cannot be in a worse situation: keep your pawns, therefore, close cemented and connected together; and it must be great strength on the other side that can overpower them.

11. Do not, though, be too much afraid of doubling*; for a double pawn is no ways disadvantageous when surrounded by three or four others. Three together are strong, but four, that make a square, with the help of other pieces, well managed, are almost invincible, and probably may produce a queen. Doubling a pawn may, also, sometimes serve to set free a piece, a rook in

---

* A pawn is said *to be doubled* when one is got before another, so as to impede the progress of the latter.

particular, which otherwise would be block-ed up, till a more advanced period of the game.

12. A pawn that has so far passed as to be no more stopped but by pieces, will in-fallibly cost a piece to hinder the making of it a queen.

13. Do not play out your pieces early in the game, because you thereby lose moves, in case your adversary can, by playing a pawn upon them, make them retire ; and at the same time it opens his game; particu-larly, do not play your queen out till your game is tolerably well opened.

14. Be careful how you play your knights at your bishop's third square, before the bi-shop's pawn has moved two squares ; because the knight proves an hinderance to it.

15. Do not crowd your game by having too many pieces together, for by so doing you may hinder the advancing or retreating your men, as occasion may require.

(B). ON CASTLING.

1. The great object in castling is, as well to render the king more secure, as to bring

the rook into play; both of which are effected by one move.

2. In general it is good play to castle your king as soon as possible: you place him in safety, and you get a rook into play by the move.

3. Sometimes it is better to play the king than to castle; as it may enable you best to attack with your pawns on that side; and when he does not castle, his bishop's second square is commonly the best place for him.

4. If your adversary should castle on the same side of the board as yourself, be cautious how you push on your pawns, leaving your king unguarded and rather make the attack with your pieces.

(C).   ON ATTACKING.

1. When your adversary plays out his pieces before he does his pawns, attack them as soon as you can with your pawns, by which you may crowd him, and make him lose moves.

2. As it is dangerous in an army to attack the enemy too soon, so do not be too hasty in pushing your pawns forwards, till they are

well sustained by one another, and also by your pieces; for if you are, you will always attack, or be attacked, at a great disadvantage: even should your attack not prove abortive, this is so essential, that you had better forego almost any advantage than deviate from it.

3. When you have brought out all your pieces, consider thoroughly your own and your adversary's game, and from his situation, and observing where he is weakest, take your resolution where to castle, and where to begin the attack; and you cannot do it in a better place than where you are the strongest, and your enemy weakest. By this method, it is very probable that you will be able to break through your adversary's game, in which some pieces must of course be exchanged.

4. While you are concerting an attack, endeavour (if it can be done consistently with it) to have your king so situated that he may castle when he pleases.

5. Never attempt to attack till you have considered what harm the adversary would be able to do you by his next moves in con-

sequence of yours, that you may prevent his designs before it be too late.

6. When the kings have castled on different sides of the board, advance upon the adversary's king the pawns you have on that side of the board, taking care to bring your pieces, especially your queen and rooks, to support them ; and the king that has castled must not move his three pawns till forced to do it.

7. Should your attack be in a prosperous way, be cautious how you are diverted from pursuing your scheme of giving mate, by taking any piece, or other advantage, your adversary may purposely throw in your way, with the intent that, by your taking that bait, he might gain a move that would make your design miscarry.

8. As long as a direct attack upon the adversary's king is unlikely to succeed, endeavour to take those of his pieces that render it so.

9. If you have moved a piece, so that your adversary drives you away with a pawn, take it for granted (generally speaking) that it is a bad move, your enemy gain-

ing that double advantage over you, of himself advancing and making you retire.

10. When the attack and defence, are thoroughly formed, and every thing prepared for the storm, if he that plays first is obliged, by the act of the person that defends, to retire, it generally ends either in the loss of the game on his side, or some very considerable disadvantage.

11. If, in pursuing a well-laid attack, you find it necessary to force your way through your adversary's defence with the loss of some pieces, and, upon counting as many moves forward as you can, you see a prospect of success, push on boldly, and sacrifice a piece or two to gain your end: these bold attempts make the finest games.

12. If the strength of your game consists in pawns, attack and take your adversary's bishops as soon as possible, because they can stop the advancing of the pawns much more than the rooks.

13. It is of consequence in the gambits to play the queen's bishop's pawn to make room for your queen, by putting her at her knight's

third square, particularly if his queen's bishop has been brought out.

14. Never attack the adversary's king without a sufficient force; and if he attacks yours without your having it in your power to retaliate, offer exchanges with him; and if he retires when you present a piece to exchange, he may lose a move by it.

15. In playing the game, endeavour to have a move, as it were, in ambuscade; that is, so to place the bishop, queen, or rook, behind a pawn, or a piece, as that upon playing that pawn or piece, you discover a check upon your adversary's king, for by this you may often get a piece, or some other advantage.

16. As the queen, rook, and bishop, operate at a distance, it is not always necessary in your attack to have them near your adversary's king; they often do better at a distance, as they cannot be drove away, and frequently, indeed, prevent your giving a stale-mate.

17. In the attack of the gambits, if once you can break the adversary's pawns on the

gambit's side your advantage becomes con-. siderable.

18. Endeavour to make yourself master of the openings, to bring the rooks into play, especially at the latter end of the game.

19. If you can ever succeed in making an opening upon your adversary's king, with two or three pawns, the game is absolutely won.

20. Always take care that your adversary's king has a move, for fear of giving a stalemate; therefore do not crowd him with your pieces, lest you inadvertently give one.

21. In the attack of gambits, in general the king's bishop is the best piece, and the king's pawn the best pawn.

(D). ON CAPTURING.

1. When you have a piece that you can take, and that cannot escape you, do not be in a hurry; see whether you can make a good move elsewhere, and take it at your leisure.

2. When you can take a man with different pieces, do not do it with the first that

occurs, but consider thoroughly with which you had best take it.

3. Where two of your adversary's pieces are *en prise*, so that you may take either, rather be determined in your choice by the value the piece is of at that particular part of the game, than by its abstract worth.

4. It is not always right to take your adversary's pawn with your king, for very often it happens to be a safeguard and protection to him.

5. When your adversary seems to have left a piece in your power, by an oversight, consider well before you take it whether it may not have been the effect of design rather than of accident, and whether he has not thereby some important move in ambush.

(E).   ON EXCHANGING.

1. Do not change without reason; it is so far from being right, that a good player will thereby spoil your situation and mend his own: but it is right altogether when you are strongest, especially by a piece (and have not an immediate checkmate in view), as then every time you change your advantage

increases; so whenever you have gained a
pawn, or any other advantage, and are not
in danger of losing the move thereby, make
as frequent exchanges of pieces as you can; or
when you have played a piece, and your adversary opposes you, then change directly,
for it is plain he wants to remove you; prevent him, therefore, and do not lose the
move.

2. Avoid, if possible, changing your
king's pawn for your adversary's king's bishop's pawn; or your queen's pawn for his
queen's bishop's pawn; because the king
and queen's pawns occupying the centre,
hinder in a great degree your adversary's
pieces from hurting you.

3. If you have a knight, supported by
two pawns, and your adversary has no pawn
to push up to remove it, he is worth a rook,
and will be so incommodious that your adversary will be forced to take it; and in
retaking him, you will have the great advantage of reuniting the two pawns.

4. Do not be too much afraid of losing
a rook for an inferior piece; for though the
rook is better than any other, except the

queen, yet it seldom comes into play, so as to operate; till the end of the game.; and it is generally better to have an inferior piece in play, than a superior outa so where the rook has not moved from his place, and the latter has made some progress in your game, an exchange may be adviseable.

5. Supposing your queen and another piece are attacked at the same time, and that, by removing your queen, you must lose the piece; if you can get two pieces in exchange for your queen, it may be sometimes adviseable rather to do so than retire.

(F).   ON GIVING OR COVERING CHECK.

1. It is not unusual to give notice on checking the queen: and as this game ought to be won by superior skill alone, without relying upon the adversary's mistakes, the player will judge for himself, whether to do it or not.

2. Checks that the adversary can easily elude are in general to be refrained from, as by them the move of the checking piece may be lost. There may, however, be cases in which checking is proper, although a mate

be not the immediate object—as, where it will force the adversary's king into a more exposed situation; where the move necessary to defend him will leave a capital piece unguarded; where the adversary's king not having castled it will force him by moving to forfeit that privilege; and where, having a piece of your own attacked, that you are not able otherwise to save, it will cause the removal of some piece that impedes his escape.

3. Never cover a check with a piece that a pawn pushed upon it may take, for fear of only getting that pawn for it.

4. If you are in a situation to give checkmate should it be your move, and your adversary, who has the move, is endeavouring to keep you in continual check, observe well the pieces he can bring upon you, in order to avoid the squares commanded by them. If the principal piece is a bishop, keep off the colour he goes on.

5. It is not impossible that while you are, as you imagine, within a move or ,two of giving checkmate, and all your pieces are employed, you may have left your king in

K

such a situation, as that your adversary may at a single move give you the mate with one of his pieces: this must be guarded against.

6. Checkmate with a knight and a bishop must be given in that corner which is of the colour the bishop moves on.

7. In order to give checkmate with a single rook, keep your king opposite the adversary's, previous to every check with the rook, as his king will then be forced to retrograde.

8. As you see the possibility of your adversary giving you checkmate, be doubly careful of every move ; a wrong 'piece moved, or a right one into a wrong square, may be fatal, though the consequence be not immediately perceived.

(G).   ON DEFENDING.

1. In the defence, you are often forced to play against the general rules, in order to break your adversary's projects, which in the attack is seldom the case.

2. After every move of the adversary, consider well what scheme he has in view, by it, and whether it has affected your own;

and if it has, do not proceed till the ill cause is removed, lest, while you are intent only on the attack, you may be yourself surprised.

3. When you have a chain of pawns, following one another, in an oblique line, strive to preserve the pawn that leads.

4. Never guard an inferior piece with a better if you can do it with a pawn, because the better piece is in that case, as it were, out of play; for the same reason do not guard a pawn with a piece, if you have it in your power to guard it with a pawn.

5. When a piece is so attacked that you cannot save it, do not run the risk of losing the game by any attempt at its preservation, but rather bestow your thoughts how to annoy your enemy in another place; for it very often happens, that, while he is running madly after a piece, you either get a pawn or two, or such a situation, as ends in his destruction.

6. Sometimes when your adversary attacks you, it is the best play to offer him an exchange; which, if he refuses, and retires, you gain at least the move of him.

7. When two of your pieces are so attacked that one of them must inevitably be lost, do not think so much of the difference of their value as on the particular effects which the capture of either may produce.

8. Prevent, if possible, the adversary getting prematurely amongst your pieces. His knights and bishops, supported by his pawns, and occasionally by his queen, may decide the game, while only half your pieces are engaged.

9. Do not suffer an adverse pawn to put *en prise* at the same time two superior pieces, which is called forking them; knights and rooks are particularly liable to be attacked in this way, the pawns not requiring to be guarded, because the situation from which they can take does not expose them to either of those pieces.

10. Let not your adversary's knight (especially if duly guarded) come to check your king and queen, or your king and rook, or your queen and rook, or your two rooks, at the same time; for in the two first cases, the king being forced to go out of check, the queen or the rook must be lost; and

in the two last cases, a rook must be lost,
at best, for a worse piece.

11. Never let your queen stand so before
your king as that your adversary, by bringing a rook or a bishop, might check your
king if she were not there ; nor behind him,
because should the rook or bishop be well
guarded, and you had no piece to interpose,
you could not avoid losing the queen for a
less valuable piece.

12. Do not let the adversary's king's bishop batter the line of your king's bishop's
pawn ; as it is the most dangerous piece to
form an attack, oppose by times your
queen's bishop to him, and get rid of him
as soon as you can.

13. When your bishop runs upon white,
endeavour to put your pawns upon black,
because your bishop then serves to prevent
your adversary's king or rook getting between them ; and so *vice versa.*

14. Strive to hinder your adversary from
doubling his rooks, particularly when there
is an opening in the game.

15. When you play your king, put him,
if possible, always upon a rank or file which

your adversary has a pawn upon, as you are thereby better covered from the rooks' ambushes.

16. When your king finds himself behind two or three pawns, and your adversary falls upon them, in order to break them or make an irruption upon your king, do not push any of them forwards till you are forced to do it.

(H).   ON CONCLUSIONS OF GAMES.

1. At the latter end of the game, remember your king is a capital piece, and do not let him be idle; it is by his means, generally, you get the move and the victory.

2. Each party having only three or four pawns on different sides of the board, and no pieces, the kings are to endeavour to gain the move. For example: if you bring your king opposite to your adversary's king, with only one house between, you will have gained the move, as your adversary cannot approach farther.

3. If you have three pawns each upon the board, and no piece, and one of yours is on one side of the board, and two on the

other, and your adversary's three pawns are opposite to your two, march with your king as fast as possible, to take his pawns ; and should his king go to support them, push on to queen with your single pawn ; and if he goes to hinder you, take his pawns, and push the others to queen.

4. When you have greatly the disadvantage of the game, having only your queen and some inferior pieces left in play, and your king happens to be in the position of stale-mate, contrive to lose the pieces, and then keep giving check to your adversary's king, always taking care not to check him where he can interpose any of his pieces that make the stale: by thus playing, you will at last force him to take your queen, and then you win the game by being in a stale-mate.

5. When you have only your king left, and your adversary has a bishop and one pawn on the rook's line, and his bishop is not of the same colour as the corner house his pawn is going to, if you can get into that corner, you cannot lose, but may win the game by a stale.

6. If you have only a bishop left against a rook, your way to insure a drawn game is to station your king on a corner square of the board, of a different colour to what the bishop goes on.

7. If one party has only the king, and the other, in addition to the king, a knight or a bishop, it must be a drawn game; and therefore next to a queen or a rook, it is best to have a pawn, from the possibility of making him a queen.

8. If your adversary has the king and a pawn, and you have only the king, endeavour to intercept the pawn; if you fail, yet, if you can get before either to the square towards which the pawn is moving, by manœuvering on the first square of that file, and the second of that and the adjoining files, you will either make a drawn game, or win by a stale.

CONCLUSION.

After all the rules that can be summed up on this truly noble game, it must at last be confessed, that without long and studious practice a proficiency must not be looked

for.   There have been, indeed, persons, who
seem to have possesed a peculiar talent herein, as wonderful as it is uncommon, and on
which, therefore, no arguments can be founded.   One thing is clear, that, (independent of
that carelessness or abstraction of mind, which
even the most sublime pursuits cannot
wholly conquer, and the influence or extent
of which may be considered matter of uncer-
tainty,) chance or luck has no share in the
victory; skill, and a consummate knowledge
of the game, will alone be *uniformly* vic-
torious.   We must not, however, yield entirely to the idea, that the best chess-player
is of necessity one of superior intellect and
capacity, since every day's experience will
shew us, that persons of otherwise very moderate talents have, and that even with an
equal degree of practice, excelled others
either of greater genius, or more sound
penetration.   We may therefore conclude,
as has been in another place remarked, that
in this, as well as in other cases, perpetual
exercise, limited in its object—mechanical
recollection of similar combinations — an
aptitude to seize on errors or want of skill

in the opponent—and though last, not least, an unabstracted attention, and unshaken command of temper, during play, are the principal causes of the knowledge of the game, and that excellence in it cannot fairly be taken as a criterion either of other faculties, or of other acquirements.

In order to place them in the most conspicuous light, and as containing the very essence of what this chapter is intended to convey, we may close it with these cautions, which may be considered, as well by the most experienced as the learner, the golden rules of Chess:

1. BEWARE OF OVERSIGHTS.

2. KEEP YOUR TEMPER; AND IF YOU CANNOT GAIN A VICTORY OVER YOUR ADVERSARY GAIN ONE OVER YOURSELF.

CHAP. IX.

PRACTICAL EXAMPLES, INTRODUCTORY TO PHILIDOR'S ANALYSIS.

———◆———

F ROM an attentive examination of Phili-dor's mode of beginning a game, we may observe the following to be his general rules.

His FIRST MOVE was *invariably* the king's pawn two squares, and the defence the same, unless in cases where he gave up the king's bishop's pawn, when he would move either the king's knight to his rook's third square, or his queen's bishop's pawn two squares.

Wh. The K. Pawn 2 sq.

Bl. The same.

His SECOND MOVE was almost as inva-riably the king's bishop to his queen's bi-shop's fourth square, in order to batter the adverse king's bishop's pawn, against which, in general, the serious attack was made.

Wh. K. Bishop at his Q. B. 4th sq.

Bl. 1. The same.　Or

　　　2. Q. B. Pawn 1 sq.　Or

　　　3. K. Knight at his B. 3d.

The THIRD MOVE was according to the second move of the black; if that was the first of the above three, then Philidor's was

Wh. Q. B. Pawn 1 sq.　If the 2d.

Wh. Q. Pawn 2 sq.　If the 3d,

Wh. Q. Pawn 1 sq.

His FOURTH MOVE was also depending on his adversary's third move: if, after Philidor's playing the first of the above three, he played his king's knight at his bishop's third square, Philidor's was

　　　Wh. Q. Pawn 2 sq.

This was generally followed by a mutual capture of the king's and queen's pawns, by which means the *white* was left with two pawns in the centre. But if instead of the knight he brought out his queen, then

　　　Wh. K. Knight at K. B. 3d sq.

If the moves went according to Philidor's second kind of third move, and the black king's pawn took his pawn, his queen would retaliate, and his king's pawn remain alone in the centre.

It is impossible to trace this farther with any degree of clearness, the learner must now, therefore, proceed with his own deductions and conclusions: he will, however, find several beginnings of games, a few pages hence, so classed, as to render the difference in them obvious, and his future progress will be founded on an attentive study of Philidor's parties.

FOOL'S MATE.

This mate is given in *two* moves only. It is so called because the mode of playing in the party who begins is highly absurd. Nevertheless, it is thought necessary to give it, to put the young player on his guard.

1.

Bl. The K. Kt. Pawn 2 sq.
Wh. The K. Pawn 1 sq.

2.

Bl. The K. B. Pawn 2 sq.
Wh. The Queen at the bl. K. R. 4th sq. and gives *checkmate*, the black king being able neither to move

out of check, nor to interpose any of his pieces.

SCHOLAR'S MATE.

The next speedy mode to the above of giving checkmate is called Scholar's Mate, and is effected as follows :

1

Wh. The K. Pawn 2 sq.

Bl. The same.

2.

Wh. The K. Bishop at the Q. B. 4th sq.

Bl. The same.

3.

Wh. The Queen at the bl. K. R. 4th sq.

Bl. The Q. Pawn 1 sq.

4.

Wh. The Q. takes the K. B. Pawn and gives *checkmate.* The black King not being able to take her on account of the white Bishop which protects her, neither can he move out nor interpose any piece in his defence.

There are many ways of evading this stratagem, which is rarely attempted except against young players; the best is as follows:.

1.

Wh. The K. Pawn 2 sq.
Bl. The same.

2.

Wh. The K. Bishop at the Q. B. 4th sq.
Bl. The same.

3.

Wh. The Queen at the bl. K. R. 4th. (*a*)
Bl. The Queen at her K. 2d.

4.

Wh. The K. Knight at his B. 3d.
Bl. The Q. Pawn 1 sq.

5.

Wh. The K. Knight at the bl. K. Kt. 4th.(*b*)
Bl. K. Kt. at his R. 3d.

6. [check.

Wh. The Bishop takes the Pawn and gives
Bl. The Knight takes the Bishop.

(*a*) In this example, the movements of the blacks rather than of the whites are proposed for imitation.

(*b*) The object of the white player having failed, he endeavours either to snatch a piece and retire, or, by the sacrifice of a knight or a bishop, still make a breach in the black pawns.

7.

Wh. The Knight takes the R. Pawn.

Bl. The Q. Knight at the Q. 2d sq.

8.

Wh. The K. R. Pawn 2 squares.

Bl. The Q. Knight at the K. B. sq.(*c*)

9.

Wh. The K. Kt. Pawn 1 sq.

Bl. The Rook takes the Knight.

10.

Wh. The Queen at her square.

If, instead of pushing the K. R. Pawn, as at the 8th couplet, the white Queen had gone to the bl. K. Knight's third square, the bl. Queen might have endeavoured at retaliation, by going to the white K. R. 4th square; the white K. Kt. Pawn would probably have advanced 1 square and the bl. Queen, would then have exchanged Queens, by first taking the Knight.

(*c*) If the knight had gone to the bishop's third square instead of the first, the white one would have taken him, and, by giving *check*, would have afforded his queen time to remove from the rook.

Other ways are—

FIRST, Instead of playing the K. Knight at his R. 3d square at the 5th move, to play *Bl.* The K. Kt. Pawn 1 sq. Then

6.
Wh. The Bishop takes the Pawn and *checks.*
Bl. The King at his Queen's sq.

7.
Wh. The Queen at her K. R. 4th.
Bl. The K. Knight at his B. 3d.

8.
Wh. The K. B. Pawn 1 sq.
Bl. The Knight takes the K. Pawn.

9.
Wh. The Pawn takes the Knight.
Bl. The K. Rook at his B. sq.

10.
Wh. The Bishop at his Q. B. 4th sq.
Bl. The K. Bishop at the white K. B. 2d square, giving *check.*

11.
Wh. The Queen takes the Bishop.
Bl. The Rook takes the Queen.

12.
Wh. The King takes the Rook.
Bl. The Queen takes the Knight, &c.

L

SECOND, Instead of playing the K. Knight at his Bishop's 3d square, as at the 7th couplet of the last example, to play the K. R. Pawn one square, and as the white Bishop will probably take the Kt. Pawn, the black Queen takes the Knight, and exchanges Queens. Should he, however, instead of taking the Kt. Pawn, give *check* with his Knight at the bl. King's 3d square, the black Q. Bishop takes him, and the Queens exchange as before.

BEGINNINGS OF GAMES.

The following first seven moves for beginnings of games, arranged as they are, so as two or four may be compared together, will greatly assist the learner ; and though it is not adviseable *merely* to get so many moves by heart, yet the so doing will enable him to begin a game without embarrassment, which is not uncommonly felt even by some experienced players.

FIRST.	SECOND.
1.	**1.**
Wh. K. P. 2 sq.	*Wh.* K. P. 2 sq.
Bl. The same.	*Bl.* The same.
2.	**2.**
K. B. at Q. B. 4th.	K. B. at Q. B. 4th.
The same.	Q. B. P. 1.
3.	**3.**
Q. B. P. 1 sq.	Q. P. 2.
K. Kt. at his B. 3d.	P. takes P.
4.	**4.**
Q. P. 2.	Q. takes P.
P. takes P.	Q. P. 1.
5.	**5.**
P. takes P.	K. B. P 2.
K. B. at Q. Kt. 3d.	Q. B. at K. 3.
6.	**6.**
Q. Kt. at his B. 3d.	K. B. at Q. 3d.
K. castles.	Q. P. 1.
7.	**7.**
K. Kt. at his K. 2d.	K. P. 1.
Q. B. P. 1 sq.	Q. B. P. 1.

THIRD.

1.
Wh. K. P. 2. sq.
Bl. The same.

2.
K. B. at Q. B. 4th.
The same.

3.
Q. B. P. 1.
Q. at K. 2d.

4.
K. Kt. at B. 3d.
The same.

5.
Q. at K. 2d.
Q. P. 1.

6.
Q. P. 1.
Q. B. P. 1.

7.
K. R. P. 1.
The same.

FOURTH.

1.
Wh. K. P. 2 sq.
Bl. The same.

2.
K. B. at Q. B. 4th.
K. Kt. at B. 3d.

3.
Q. P. 1.
K. B. at Q. B. 4th.

4.
K. Kt. at B. 3d.
Q. P. 1.

5.
Q. B. P. 1.
King castles.

6.
Q. R. P. 2.
The same.

7.
King castles.
Q. B. at K. 3.

FIFTH.	SIXTH.
1.	**1.**
Wh. K. P. 2. sq.	*Wh.* K. P. 2 sq,
Bl. The same.	*Bl.* The same.
2.	**2.**
K. B. at Q. B. 4th.	K. B. at Q. B. 4th.
Q. B. P. 1.	The same.
3.	**3.**
Q. P. 2.	Q. B. P. 1.
K. P. takes P,!	K. Kt. at B. 3d.
4.	**4.**
Q. takes P.	Q. P. 2.
Q. P. 1.	P. takes P.
5.	**5.**
K. B. P. 2.	P. takes P.
Q. B. at K. 3d.	K. B. gives *check*.
6.	**6.**
B. takes B.	Q. B. covers.
P. takes B.	B. takes B.
7.	**7.**
Q. B. P. 2.	Q. Kt. takes B.
Q. P. 1.	Q. P. 2.

SEVENTH.	EIGHTH.

1.

Wh. K. P. 2 sq.
Bl. The same.

1.

Wh. K. P. 2 sq.
Bl. Q. B. P. 2.

2.

K. B. at Q. B. 4th.
The same.

2.

K. B. P. 2.
Q. Kt. at B. 3d.

3.

Q. B. P. 1.
Q. at K. B. 3d.

3.

K. Kt. at B. 3d.
K. P. 1.

4.

K. Kt. at B. 3d.
Q. Kt. at B. 3d.

4.

Q. B. P. 1.
Q. P. 2.

5.

Q. Kt. P. 2.
K. B. at Q. Kt. 3d.

5.

K. P. 1.
K. B. P 2.

6.

Q. R. P. 2.
Q. R. P. 1.

6.

Q. P. 2.
K. Kt. at K. R. 3d.

7.

Q. P. 1.
The same.

7.

Q. B. at K. 3d.
Q. at her Kt. 3d.

NINTH.

1.
Wh. K. P. 2 sq.
Bl. The same.

2.
K. Kt. at B. 3.
Q. P. 1.

3.
K. B. at Q. B. 4th.
K. B. P. 2.

4.
Q. P. 1.
Q. B. P. 1.

5.
P. takes P.
B. takes P.

6.
Q. B. at wh. K. Kt. 4th.
K. Kt. at B. 3d.

7.
Q. Kt. at Q. 2d.
Q. P. 1.

TENTH.

1.
Wh. K. P. 2 sq.
Bl. The same.

2.
Q. B. P. 1.
Q. P. 2.

3.
P. takes P.
Q. takes P.

4.
Q. P. 1.
K. B. P. 2.

5.
K. B. P. 2.
K. P. 1.

6.
Q. P. 1.
Q. at K. B. 2d.

7.
Q. B. at K. 3d.
K. Kt. at K. B. 3d.

In these the black only are recommended for imitation.

FIRST.	SECOND.
1.	**1.**
Wh. K. P. 2 sq.	*Wh.* K. P. 2 sp.
Bl. The same.	*Bl.* The same.
2.	**2.**
K. B. P. 2.	K. B. P. 2.
P. takes P.	P. takes P.
3.	**3.**
K. Kt. at his B. 3d.	K. B. at his Q. B. 4th.
K. Kt. P. 2.	Q. gives *check*.
4.	**4.**
K. B. at his Q. B. 4th.	K. at his B. sq.
K. B. at his Kt. 2d.	K. Kt. P. 2.
5.	**5.**
K. R. P. 2.	K. Kt. at his B. 3d.
K. R. P. 1.	Q. at her K. R. 4.
6.	**6.**
Q. P. 2.	Q. P. 2.
Q. P. 1.	Q. P. 1.
7.	**7.**
Q. B. P. 1.	Q. B. P. 1.
The same.	Q. B. at wh. K. Kt. 4th.

THIRD.	FOURTH.
1.	**1.**
Wh. K. P. 2 sq.	*Wh.* K. P. 2 sq.
Bl. The same.	*Bl.* The same.
2.	**2.**
K. B. P. 2.	K. B. P. 2.
Q. P. 2.	P. takes P.
3.	**3.**
K. P. takes P.	K. Kt. at his B. 3d.
Q. takes P.	K. B. at K. 2d.
4.	**4.**
P. takes P.	K. B. at his Q. B. 4th.
Q. takes P. and *checks.*	K. B. gives *check.*
5.	**5.**
B. covers.	K. Kt. P. 1.
K. B. at Q. 3d.	P. takes P.
6.	**6.**
K. Kt. at his B. 3d.	K. castles.
Q. at K. 2d.	P. tks. P. & gives *ch.*
7.	**7.**
Q. P. 2.	K. at K. R. sq.
Q. B. at K. 3d.	K. B. at his 3d.

FIFTH.	SIXTH.
1.	**1.**
Wh. K. P. 2 sq.	*Wh.* Q. P. 2 sq.
Bl. The same.	*Bl.* The same.
2.	**2.**
K. B. P. 2.	Q. B. P. 2.
P. takes P.	P. takes P.
3.	**3.**
K. Kt. at his B. 3d.	K. P. 2 sq.
K. Kt. P. 2.	The same.
4.	**4.**
K. B. at Q. B. 4th.	Q. P. 1.
K. Kt. P. 1.	K. B. P. 2.
5.	**5.**
K. Kt. at *bl.* K. 4th	Q. Kt. at his B. 3d.
Q. gives *check*.	K. Kt. at his B. 3d.
6.	**6.**
K. at his B. sq.	K. B. P. 1.
K. Kt. at his B. 3d.	K. B. at Q. B. 4th.
7.	**7.**
Q. at K. sq.	Q. Kt. at R. 4th.
Q. P. 2 sq.	B. takes the K. Kt.

A SPEEDY CHECKMATE,

Owing to the Black playing out his Kt. Pawn too soon.

1.

Wh. The K. Pawn 2 squares.
Bl. ·The same.

2.

Wh. The Q. Pawn 1 sq.
Bl. The K. Kt. 1 sq.

3

Wh. The K. Knight at K. B. 3d sq.
Bl. The K. B. Pawn 2 sq.

4.

Wh. The K. Pawn takes the Pawn.
Bl. The K. Kt. Pawn takes the Pawn.

5.

Wh. The K. Knight takes the K. Pawn.
Bl. The Q. Pawn 1 sq.

6.

Wh. Queen gives *check* at the bl. K. R. 4th.
Bl. The King at his 2d sq. having no other.

7.

Wh. Queen gives *ch.-mate* at the bl. K. B. 2d.

GAMES FROM THE CALABROIS.

FIRST.

1.

Wh. The K. Pawn 2. sq.
Bl. The same.

2.

Wh. The K. Knight at his B. 3d sq.
Bl. The Q. Kt. at his B. 3d sq.

3.

Wh. The K. Bishop at the Q. B. 4th sq.
Bl. The same.

4.

Wh. The Q. B. Pawn 1 sq.
Bl. The K. Knight at the K. B. 3d sq.

5.

Wh. The Q. Pawn 2 sq.
Bl. The K. Pawn takes the Pawn.

6.

Wh. The Pawn takes the Pawn.
Bl. K. Bishop gives *ch.* at wh. Q. Kt. 4th sq.

7.

Wh. Q. Knight covers the *check* at his B. 3d.
Bl. The K. Knight takes the K. Pawn.

8.

Wh. The King castles with K. R.
Bl. The K. Knight takes the Q. Knight.

9.

Wh. The Pawn takes the K. Knight.
Bl. The K. Bishop takes the Pawn.

10.

Wh. The Queen at her Knight's 3d sq.
Bl. The K. Bishop takes the Q. Rook.

11.

Wh. The K. Bishop takes the K. B. Pawn
and gives *check*.

Bl. The King at his Bishop's sq.

12.

Wh. The Q. Bishop at the bl. K. Kt. 4th sq.

Bl. The Q. Knight at the King's 2d sq.

13.

Wh. The K. Knight at the bl. K. 4th sq.

Bl. The Q. Pawn 2 sq.

14.

Wh. The Queen at the K. B. 8d sq.

Bl. The Q. Bishop at the K. B. 4th sq.

15.

Wh. The K. Bishop at the bl. K. 3d sq.

Bl. The K. Kt. Pawn 1 sq.

16.

Wh. Q. B. gives *check* at the K. R. 3d sq.

Bl. The King at his own square.

17.

Wh. The K. Bishop gives *checkmate* at the
bl. K. B. 2d sq.

SECOND.

1.

Wh. The K. Pawn two sq.

Bl. The K. Pawn one sq.

2.

Wh. The Q. Pawn 2 sq.
Bl. The K. Knight at his B. 3d sq.

9.

Wh. The K. Bishop at his Q. 3d sq.
Bl. The Q. Knight at his B. 3d sq.

4.

Wh. The K. Knight at his B. 3d.
Bl. The K. Bishop at his K. 2d sq.

5.

Wh. The K. R. Pawn 2 sq.
Bl. The King castles.

6.

Wh. The K. Pawn one sq.
Bl. The K. Knight at his Q. 4th sq.

7.

Wh. K. B. takes the K. R. P. and gives *check*.
Bl. The King takes the K. Bishop.

8.

Wh. K. Kt. gives *check* at the bl. K. Kt. 4th.
Bl. The King at his Kt. 3d sq.

9.

Wh. The K. R. Pawn gives *check*.
Bl. The King at his B. 4th.

10.

Wh. K. Kt. Pawn 2 sq. and gives *checkmate*.

THIRD.

1.

Wh. The K. Pawn 2 sq.

Bl. The Q. Kt. Pawn one sq.

2.

Wh. The Q. Pawn 2 sq.

Bl. The Q. Bishop at his Kt. 2d.

3.

Wh. The K. Bishop at his Q. 3d.

Bl. The K. B. Pawn 2 sq.

4.

Wh. The Pawn takes the Pawn.

Bl. The Q. Bishop takes K. Kt. Pawn.

5.

Wh. Queen gives *check* at the bl. K. R. 4th.

Bl. The K. Kt. Pawn covers.

6.

Wh. The Pawn takes the Pawn.

Bl. The K. Knight at his B. 3d.

7.

Wh. Pawn takes the P. discovering *check.*

Bl. The Knight takes the Queen.

8.

Wh. Bishop gives *checkmate* at the bl. Kt. 3d.

FOURTH.

1.

Wh. The K. Pawn 2 sq.

Bl. The same.

2.

Wh. The K. B. Pawn 2 sq.
Bl. The Pawn takes the Pawn.

3.

Wh. The K. Kt. at his B. 3d sq.
Bl. The K. R. Pawn one sq.

4.

Wh. The K. Bishop at the Q. B. 4th sq.
Bl. The K. Kt. Pawn 2 sq.

5.

Wh. The K. R. Pawn 2 sq.
Bl. The K. B. Pawn one sq.

6.

Wh. The K. Kt. takes the K. Kt. Pawn.
Bl. The K. B. Pawn takes the Knight.

7.

Wh. Queen gives *check* at the bl. K. B. 4th.
Bl. The King at his 2d.

8.

Wh. Queen gives *check* at the bl. K. B. 2d.
Bl. The King at his Q. 3d.

9.

Wh. Queen gives *check* at the bl. Q. 4th.
Bl. The King at his 2d.

10.

Wh. Queen gives *checkmate* at the bl. K. 4th.

CHESS ANALYSED:

OR

INSTRUCTIONS,

BY WHICH

A PERFECT KNOWLEDGE

OF THIS

NOBLE GAME

MAY

IN A SHORT TIME BE ACQUIRED.

BY

A. D. PHILIDOR.

FROM THE LAST EDITION CORRECTED BY THE AUTHOR.

ADVERTISEMENT.

MR. PHILIDOR in his early editions used initial letters only in his games, a practice which he corrected in the later ones, by putting the words at length. In this he has been followed by other writers on the subject. I have adopted a method between both, having put the pieces moved or taken in words at length, but the descriptive words in initials only: and I flatter myself that it will be found productive of greater facility in playing the games, since the piece alluded to will be more easily discovered.

In the notes references are made to the elementary rules, instead of their being printed over again. It is hoped, that the avoiding repetition will not be the sole advantage resulting from this mode, since it is adopted under the idea of fixing the rules, by reference to them, more firmly in the learner's memory.

The Edition from which this is printed is that of 1791, where Philidor first added some important remarks, particularly on the back games.

The Reader is addressed as the player of the whites, and the player of the blacks in the third person.

(☞) Shews that from this move a back game commences.

PHILIDOR'S ANALYSIS.

FIRST PARTY,

WITH

TWO BACK GAMES.

1.

Wh. T HE K. Pawn 2 sq.
Bl. The same.

2.

Wh. The K. Bishop at his Q. B. 4th. sq.
Bl. The same.

3.

Wh. The Q. B. Pawn one sq.
Bl. The K. Knight at his B. 3d sq.

4.

Wh. The Q. Pawn two sq. (*a*)
Bl. The Pawn takes it.

(*a*) This pawn is played, first to hinder your adversary's king's bishop playing upon your king's bishop's pawn ; and secondly, to get the strength of your pawns into the middle of the board.

5.

Wh. The Pawn takes the Pawn. (*b*)

Bl. The K. Bishop at his Q. Kt. 3d sq. (*c*)

6.

Wh. The Q. Knight at his B. 3d sq.

Bl. The King castles.

7.

Wh. The K. Knight at his K. 2d sq. (*d*)

Bl. The Q. B. Pawn one sq.

8.

Wh. The K. Bishop at his Q. 3d. sq. (*e*)

Bl. The Q. Pawn 2 sq.

(*b*) When you have two pawns in this situation, push neither before your adversary proposes to exchange, according to Rule A. 6, and see A. 4.

(*c*) If he had given you check with it, you would cover the check with your bishop, in order to take his with your knight, in case he took yours; your knight would then defend your king's pawn, otherwise unguarded. Probably he will not take your bishop, because a good player strives to keep his king's bishop as long as possible.

(*d*) Do not play him at the bishop's third square.—See Rule A. 14.

(*e*) He retires to avoid being attacked by the black queen's pawn, which would force you to take his pawn with yours; this would weaken your game, and spoil the project of getting your pawns into the centre.

9.

Wh. The K. Pawn one sq.

Bl. The K. Knight at his K. sq.

10.

Wh. The Q. Bishop at his K. 3d sq.

Bl. The K. B. Pawn one sq. *(f)*

11.

Wh. The Queen at her 2d sq. *(g)*

Bl. The K. B. Pawn takes the Pawn. *(h)*

12.

Wh. The Q. Pawn takes the Pawn.

Bl. The Q. Bishop at his K. 3d. sq. *(i)* ☜

(*f*) To give an opening to his king's rook ; and this you cannot hinder, whether you take his pawn or not.

(*g*) You would have done wrong in taking the pawn offered to you, because your king's pawn would then lose · its line ; whereas, if he takes it, that of your queen supplies the place, and you may afterwards sustain it with your king's bishop's pawn. These two pawns will probably win the game, because they can now no more be separated without the loss of a piece, or one of them will make a queen. You play your queen there to support your king's bishop's pawn, and your queen's bishop, which, being taken, would otherwise oblige you to take his bishop with the pawn ; and thus your best pawns would have been divided ; and the game lost.

(*h*) To give an opening to his king's rook.

(*i*) To protect his queen's pawn, and with a view of pushing that of his queen's bishop. He might have

13.

Wh. The K. Knight at his K. B. 4th sq. (*k*)
Bl. The Queen at her K. 2d sq.

14.

Wh. The Q. Bishop takes the Bishop. (*l*)
Bl. The Pawn takes the Bishop.

15.

Wh. The King castles with his Rook. (*m*)
Bl. The Q. Knight at his Q. 2d. sq.

16.

Wh. The Knight takes the Bishop.
Bl. The Queen takes the Knight.

---

taken your bishop without prejudice to his scheme, but he prefers your taking his, in order to get an opening for his queen's rook, though he has his knight's pawn doubled by it; but see Rule A. 11. This will be the subject of the first back game: the black bishop will there take your bishop; and it will be seen, that, with equal good play, it will make no difference. The king's pawn, together with the queen's, or the king's bishop's pawn, well played, and well sustained, will certainly win the game.

N.B. These back games will be only on the most essential moves; for, otherwise, they would be innumerable.

(*k*) Your king's pawn being as yet in no danger, your knight attacks his bishop, in order to take him, or have him removed.

(*l*) See Rule G. 12.

(*m*) You castle on this side, in order to protect your king's bishop's pawn; which push two squares as soon as your king's pawn is attacked.

17.

Wh. The K· B. Pawn 2 sq.

Bl. The K. Knight at his Q. B. 2d. sq.

18.

Wh. The Q. Rook at its K. sq.

Bl. The K. Kt. Pawn one sq. (*n*)

19.

Wh. The K. R. Pawn one sq. (*o*)

Bl. The Q. Pawn one sq·

20.

Wh. The Knight at his K. 4th. sq.

Bl. The K. R. Pawn one sq. (*p*)

21.

Wh. The Q. Kt. Pawn one sq.

Bl. The Q. R. Pawn one sq.

22.

Wh. The K. Kt. Pawn 2 sq.

Bl. The K. Knight at his Q. 4th sq.

23.

Wh. The Knight at his K. Kt. 3d sq. (*q*)

Bl. The K. Knight at the wh. K. 3d sq. (*r*)

(*n*) To hinder you from pushing your king's bishop's pawn upon his queen.

(*o*) In order to unite all your pawns together, and push them afterwards with vigour.

(*p*) To hinder your knight entering in his game, and forcing his queen to remove ; were he to play otherwise, your pawns would have an open field.

(*q*) To enable yourself to push your king's bishop's

24.

Wh. The Q. Rook takes the Knight.

Bl. The Pawn takes the Rook.

25.

Wh. The Queen takes the Pawn.

Bl. The Q. Rook takes the R. Pawn.

26.

Wh. The Rook at the K. sq. (*s*)

Bl. The Queen takes the Q. Kt. Pawn.

27.

Wh. The Queen at her K. 4th sq.

Bl. The Queen at her K. 3d sq. (*t*)

28.

Wh. The K. B. Pawn one sq.

Bl. The Pawn takes it.

29.

Wh. The Pawn takes the Pawn. (*u*)

---

pawn next; it will then be supported by the bishop, rook, knight, and pawn, while he has only the queen, rook, and pawn bearing on it.

(*r*) He plays thus to hinder your project, by breaking the strength of your pawns, which he would do by pushing the king's knight's pawn; but you prevent it, by exchanging you rook for his knight.

(*s*) To protect your king's pawn when you push your king's bishop's pawn.

(*t*) The queen returns to hinder the checkmate, now ready prepared.

(*u*) Otherwise your project, laid in the beginning

Bl. The Queen at her 4th sq. (*w*)

30.

Wh. The Queen takes the Queen.

Bl. The Pawn takes the Queen.

31.

Wh. The Bishop takes the Pawn in his way.

Bl. The Knight at his 3d sq.

32.

Wh. The K. B. Pawn one sq. (*x*)

Bl. The Q. Rook at the wh. Q. Kt. 2d sq.

33.

Wh. The Bishop at his Q. 3d sq.

Bl. The King at his B. 2d sq.

34.

Wh. Bishop at the bl. K. B. 4th sq. (*y*)

Bl. The Knight at the wh. Q. B. 4th sq.

35.

Wh. The Knight at the bl. K. R. 4th sq.

Bl. The K. Rook gives *check.*

---

would be abandoned, and you would run the risk of losing the game.

(*w*) He offers to change queens to spoil your scheme of giving him checkmate with your queen and bishop.

(*x*) See Rule G. 13.

(*y*) Here is an example of the above Rule : If your bishop was black, your adversary's king might get in between the two pawns.

36.

Wh. The Bishop at his Kt. 4th sq.

Bl. The Knight at the wh. Q. 2d. sq.

37.

Wh. The K. Pawn gives *check.*

Bl. The King at his Kt. 3d sq. (*z*) ☜

38.

Wh. The K. B. Pawn one sq.

Bl. The Rook at his K. B. sq.

39.

Wh. Knight gives *check* at his K. B. 4th sq.

Bl. The King at his Kt. 2d sq.

40.

Wh. The Bishop at the bl. K. R. 4th sq.

Bl. Plays any where; the white pushes to Queen.

FIRST BACK GAME,

Or Continuation of the 1st *Game from the* 12th *Couplet.*

12.

Wh. The Q. Pawn takes the Pawn.

Bl. The K. Bishop takes the Q. Bishop.

(*z*). As his king may retire to his bishop's square, it is made the subject of the second back game, which will shew you how to proceed in that case.

13.

Wh. The Queen takes the Bishop.
Bl. The Q. Bishop at his K. 3d sq.

14.

Wh. The K. Knight at his K. B. 4th sq.
Bl. The Queen at her K. 2d sq.

15.

Wh. The Knight takes the Bishop.
Bl. The Queen takes the Knight.

16.

Wh. The King castles with his Rook.
Bl. The Q. Knight at his Q. 2d sq.

17.

Wh. The K. B. Pawn 2 sq.
Bl. The K. Kt. Pawn one sq.

18.

Wh. The K. R. Pawn one sq.
Bl. The K. Knight at his 2d sq.

19.

Wh. The K. Kt. Pawn 2 sq.
Bl. The Q. B. Pawn one sq.

20.

Wh. The Knight at his K. 2d sq.
Bl. The Q. Pawn one sq.

21.

Wh. The Queen at her 2d sq.
Bl. The Q. Knight at his 3d sq.

22.

Wh. The Knight at his K. Kt. 3d sq.
Bl. The Q. Knight at his Q. 4th sq.

23.

Wh. The Q. Rook at its K. sq.
Bl. The Q. Knight at the wh. K. 3d sq.

24.

Wh. The Rook takes the Knight.
Bl. The Pawn takes the Rook.

25.

Wh. The Queen takes the Pawn.
Bl. The Queen takes the Q. R. Pawn.

26.

Wh. The K. B. Pawn one sq.
Bl. The Queen takes the Q. Kt. Pawn.

27.

Wh. The K. B. Pawn one sq.
Bl. The Knight at his K. sq.

28.

Wh. The K. Kt. Pawn one sq.
Bl. The Queen at the wh. Q. 4th sq.

29.

Wh. The Queen takes the Queen.
Bl. The Pawn takes the Queen.

30.

Wh. The K. Pawn one sq.
Bl. The Knight at his Q. 3d sq.

31.

Wh. The Knight at his K. 4th sq.

Bl. The Knight at his K. B. 4th. sq.

32.

Wh. The Rook takes the Knight.

Bl. The Pawn takes the Rook.

33.

Wh. The Knight at the bl. Q. 3d sq.

Bl. The K. B. Pawn one sq. or any where, the game being lost.

34.

Wh. The K. Pawn one sq.

Bl. The K. Rook at his Q. Kt. sq.

35.

Wh. The Bishop gives *check.*

Bl. King at his R. sq. having but one place.

36.

Wh. The Knight gives *check.*

Bl. The King at his Kt. sq.

37.

Wh. Knight at the bl. Q. sq. discovering *check*

Bl. The King at his R. sq.

38.

Wh. The K. Pawn making a Queen gives *checkmate.*

SECOND BACK GAME.

37.

Wh. The K. Pawn gives *check.*
Bl. The King at his B. sq.

38.

Wh. The Rook at his Q. R. sq.
Bl. The Rook gives *check* at wh. Q. Kt. sq.

39.

Wh. The Rook takes the Rook.
Bl. The Knight takes the Rook.

40.

Wh. The King at his R. 2d sq.
Bl. The Knight at the wh. Q. B. 3d sq.

41.

Wh. The Knight at his K. B. 4th sq.
Bl. The Knight at the wh. K. 4th sq.

42.

Wh. The Knight takes the Pawn.
Bl. The Rook at his K. Kt. fourth sq.

43.

Wh. The K. Pawn gives *check.*
Bl. The King at his B. 2d sq.

44.

Wh. Bishop gives *check* at the bl. K. 3d sq.
Bl. The King takes the Bishop.

45.

Wh. The K. Pawn makes a Queen, and wins.

SECOND PARTY,

WITH

THREE BACK GAMES.

1.

Wh. T HE K. Pawn 2 sq.

Bl. The same.

2.

Wh. The K. Bishop at his Q. B. 4th sq.

Bl. The Q. B. Pawn one sq.

3.

Wh. The Q. Pawn 2 sq. (*a*)

Bl. The Pawn takes the Pawn. (*b*)

(*a*) Playing any thing else would give your adversary the move, and consequently the attack; this would put your game in a bad condition, because you could no longer hinder him from puting the strength of his pawns in the middle of the board, and (supposing equally good play) winning the game.

(*b*) If he refuses taking your pawn, in order to pursue his scheme of attacking your bishop with his queen's pawn, he will (with good play on both sides) lose the game, because his queen's pawn being separated from his comrades must be lost. This producing great alterations in the game, is the subject of the first back game.

4.

Wh. The Queen takes the Pawn.
Bl. The Q. Pawn one sq.

5.

Wh. The K. B. Pawn 2 sq.
Bl. The Q. Bishop at his K. 3d. sq. (*c*)

6.

Wh. The K. Bishop at his Q. 3d sq.
Bl. The Q. Pawn one sq.

7.

Wh. The K. Pawn one sq.
Bl. The Q. B. Pawn one sq.

8.

Wh. The Queen at her K. B. 2d sq.
Bl. The Q. Knight at his Q. B. 3d sq.(*d*)

9.

Wh. The Q. B. Pawn one sq.
Bl. The K. Kt. Pawn one sq.

10.

Wh. The K. R. Pawn one sq.

(*c*) He plays this bishop, first to push his queen's pawn, in order to make room for his king's bishop; secondly, to oppose it to your king's bishop; and thirdly, to get rid of him—according to Rule G. 12.

(*d*) If instead of getting out his pieces he should continue to push on his pawns, he would lose the game; see Rule A. 7. This will be shewn by a second back game, which will demonstrate the truth of Rule A. 8.

Bl. The K. R. Pawn 2 sq. (*e*)

        11.

Wh. The K. Kt. Pawn one sq. (*f*)

Bl. The K. Knight at his R. 3d sq.

        12.

Wh. The K. Knight at his B. 3d sq.

Bl. The K. Bishop at his K. 2d sq.

        13.

Wh. The Q. R. Pawn 2 sq.

Bl. The K. Knight at his B. 4th sq.

        14.

Wh. The King at his B. sq. (*g*)

Bl. The K. R. Pawn one sq.

(*e*) To hinder your pawns' (being four to three) falling upon his. There are two equal bodies of pawns on the board: you have four to three on your king's side, and he on his queen's side; those on the king's side have always some advantage, the king being by a superior number better guarded: nevertheless, he that is able first to separate his adversary's pawns (especially on that side where they are strongest) will win the game.

(*f*) This is a material move; had you not made it, he would, by pushing his king's rook's pawn one square, have immediately cut off the communication between your pawns, as your king's knight's pawn could not have joined that of your bishop, without being liable to be taken by his rook's pawn *en passant*.

(*g*) In order to be able to form your attack, as well on your left as on your right wing.

15.

Wh. The K. Kt. Pawn one sq.
Bl. The Knight *checks* the King and Rook.

16.

Wh. The King at his Kt. 2d sq.
Bl. The Knight takes the Rook.

17.

Wh. The King takes the Knight. (*h*)
Bl. The Queen at her 2d sq.

18.

Wh. The Queen at her K. Kt. sq. (*i*)
Bl. The Q. R. Pawn 2 sq.

19.

Wh. The Q. Bishop at his K. 3d sq. (*k*)
Bl. The Q. Kt. Pawn one sq.

(*h*) Though you lose a superior for an inferior piece, yet this change turns to your advantage; see Rule E. 4. Besides, his knight proves very troublesome to you; and the taking him puts your king in an easy situation, and enables you the better to form your attack on which ever side your adversary shall castle.

(*i*) To sustain your king's bishop's pawn, lest he should sacrifice his bishop for your two pawns, which he would certainly do; because the strength of your game consisting in your pawns, the breaking of them would give him the attack, and probably make you lose the game.

(*k*) To draw him to push his queen's bishop's pawn,

20.

Wh. The Q. Knight at his R. 3d. sq

Bl. The King castles with his Q. Rook. (*l*)

21.

Wh. The K. Bishop gives *check.*

Bl. The King at his Q. B. 2d sq.

22.

Wh. The Q. Knight at his Q. B. 2d sq. (*m*)

Bl. The Q. Rook at her own place.

23.

Wh. The K. Bishop at the bl. Q. Kt. 4th sq.

Bl. The Queen at her own sq. (*n*)

24.

Wh. The Q. Kt. Pawn 2 sq.

Bl. The Queen at her K. B. sq.

25.

Wh. The Q. Kt. Pawn takes the Q. B. Pawn.

Bl. The Q. Kt. Pawn takes the Pawn.

---

which would give you the game very soon, because it enables your knights to enter his game every where.

(*l*) He castles on this side, to avoid the great strength of your pawns on the other, particularly as they are already farther advanced on that side.

(*m*) If, instead of going back, in order to pursue your attack on the pawns that retard your winning of the game, you should give him check, you would lose at least two moves by it.

(*n*) With a design to put her next at her king's bi-

26.

Wh. The K. Knight at his Q. 2d sq. (*o*)

Bl. The Q. B. Pawn one sq. (*p*) ♘

27.

Wh. The K. Knight at his B. 3d sq.

Bl. The K. B. Pawn one sq. (*q*)

28.

Wh. The Q. Bishop gives *check*.

Bl. The King at his Q. Kt. 2d sq.

29.

Wh. K. Bishop takes the Knight and *checks*.

Bl. The King takes the Bishop.

30.

Wh. The K. Knight gives *check*.

Bl. The King at his Q. 2d sq. (*r*)

---

shop's square, foreseeing that his whole game depends on sustaining his queen's bishop's pawn.

(*o*) To attack the pawn in question.

(*p*) Equally to gain one move, and to hinder your king's knight from placing himself at your queen's knight's third square.

(*q*) Whatever he may play now, the game is irre-trievable; because as soon as your knights can get a free passage it is lost.

(*r*) If his king takes your queen's bishop, you have his queen by a discovered check upon him; and if he plays otherwise, he loses his queen's bishop.

31.

Wh. The K. B. Pawn one sq.

Bl. The Q. Bishop at his K. Kt. sq.

32.

Wh. The K. Pawn gives *check.*

Bl. The King at his home.

33.

Wh. The K. Knight at the bl. Q. Kt. 4th sq.

Bl. The K. Bishop at his Q. 3d sq.

34.

Wh. The Queen at her 4th sq. (*s*)

Bl. Lost every where

FIRST BACK GAME.

3

Wh. The Q. Pawn 2 sq.

Bl. The same.

4.

Wh. The K. Pawn takes the Pawn.

Bl. The Q. B. Pawn takes the Pawn.

5.

Wh. The K. Bishop gives *check.*

Bl. The Q. Bishop covers the *check.*

(*s*) The queen afterwards takes his queen's pawn, enters his game, and masters most of his pieces.

6.

Wh. The Bishop takes the Bishop.

Bl. The Knight takes the Bishop.

7.

Wh. The Q. Pawn takes the Pawn.

Bl. The Knight takes the Pawn.

8.

Wh. The Queen at her K. 2d sq.

Bl. The same.

9.

Wh. The Q. Knight at his B. 3d sq.

Bl. The King castles.

10.

Wh. The Bishop at his K. B. 4th sq.

Bl. The Q. Knight at his B. 3d sq.

11.

Wh. The King castles.

Bl. The Queen takes the Queen.

12.

Wh. The K. Knight takes the Queen.

Bl. The Q. Pawn one sq.

13.

Wh. The Q. Knight at his K. 4th sq.

Bl. The K. B. Pawn one sq. (*a*)

(*a*) If he had played his rook at his king's square to attack your two knights, you might have let him take

14.

Wh. The K. R. Pawn 2 sq.

Bl. The same.

15.

Wh. The K. Rook at its 3d sq.

Bl. The K. Knight at his R. 3d sq.

16.

Wh. The Bishop takes the Knight.

Bl. The Rook takes the Bishop.

17.

Wh. The K. Rook at its Q. 3d sq.

Bl. The Q. Rook at its K. sq.

18.

Wh. The K. Knight takes the Pawn.

Bl. The Knight at the wh. Q. Kt. 4th sq. (*b*)

19.

Wh. The K. Rook at its K. 3d sq.

Bl. Knight takes the R. Pawn and *checks*.

20.

Wh. The King at his Q. Kt. sq.

Bl. The Knight at the wh. Q. Kt. 3d sq.

---

the knight that is at your king's second square, and with your other have attacked his king's bishop's pawn: the consequence is plainly seen.

(*b*) Had he taken your knight with his rook, your knight (taking his again) would have gained you his king's bishop by a check given with your rook, and consequently the game.

21.

Wh. Q. Knight *checks* the King & Rook. (*c*)

SECOND BACK GAME.

8.

Wh. The Queen at her K. B. 2d sq.
Bl. The Q. B. Pawn one sq.

9.

Wh. The K. Bishop at his K. 2d sq.
Bl. The Q. Pawn one sq.

10.

Wh. The Q. B. Pawn one sq.
Bl. The Q. Pawn one sq.

11.

Wh. The K. Bishop at his 3d sq.
Bl. The Q. Bishop at the Q. 4th sq.

12.

Wh. The Q. Kt. Pawn one sq.
Bl. The Q. Kt. Pawn 2 sq.

13.

Wh. The Q. R. Pawn 2 sq.*
Bl. The Q. B. Pawn takes the Pawn.

(*c*) Having the advantage of a good situation, and a rook for a bishop, he must get the game. This shews that when both sides play well he that moves first will almost always win.

* Quære. The *King's* R. Pawn? *Ed.*

14.

Wh. The Q. R. Pawn takes the Pawn.

Bl. The Q. Bishop takes the K. Bishop.

15.

Wh. The K. Knight takes the Bishop.

Bl. The Q. Knight at his Q. 2d sq.

16.

Wh. The Q. Bishop at his K. 3d sq.

Bl. The Rook at its Q. Kt. sq.

17.

Wh. The Q. B. Pawn one sq.

Bl. The Q. Knight at his 3d sq.

18.

Wh. The Q. Knight at his Q. 2d sq.

Bl. The K. Bishop at the wh. Q. Kt. 4th.

19.

Wh. The King castles. (*a*)

THIRD BACK GAME,

26.

Wh. The K. Knight at his Q. 2d. sq.

Bl. The K. B. Pawn one sq.

(*a*) He will undoubtedly win the game, because all his pawns are well situated, and well sustained; whilst his adversary's pawns are separated, and likely to be lost.

27.

Wh. The K. Knight at his Q. Kt. 3d sq.

Bl. The Q. B. Pawn one sq.

28.

Wh. The Q. Bishop gives *check.*

Bl. The King at his Q. Kt. 2d sq.

29.

Wh. The K. Kt. *checks* at the bl. Q. B. 4th sq.

Bl. The K. Bishop takes the Knight.

30.

Wh. The Q. Bishop takes the Bishop.

Bl. The Queen at her B. sq.

31.

Wh. The Rook at his Q. Kt. sq.

Bl. The King at his Q. B. 2d sq.

32.

Wh. The Q. Bishop *checks* at the bl. Q. 3d sq.

Bl. The King at his Q. sq.

33.

Wh. Queen *checks* at the bl. Q. Kt. 3d sq.

Bl. The King any where, loses the game.

THIRD PARTY,

WITH

THREE BACK GAMES.

BEGINNING WITH THE BLACK.

1.

Bl. THE K. Pawn 2 sq.
Wh. The same.

2.

Bl. The K. Knight at his B. 3d sq.
Wh. The Q. Pawn one sq.

3.

Bl. The K. Bishop at the Q. B. 4th sq.
Wh. The K. B. Pawn 2 sq. (*a*)

---

* By this party it is shewn, that playing the king's knight the second move is entirely wrong, because it not only loses the attack, but gives it to the adversary. It will be seen likewise by three back games, that a good attack keeps the defender always embarrassed.

(*a*) Any thing else your adversary could have played this was your best move, it being advantageous to change your king's bishop's pawn for his king's pawn; because your royal pawns place themselves in the middle of the board, and stop the progress of your adversary's pieces; besides, you gain the attack upon him, and that

4.

Bl. The Q. Pawn one sq.

Wh. The Q. B. Pawn one sq.

5.

Bl. The K. Pawn takes the Pawn (*b*) ☞

Wh. The Q. Bishop takes the Pawn.

6.

Bl. The Q. Bishop at the wh. K. Kt. 4th sq.

Wh. The K. Knight at his B. 3d sq. (*c*)

7.

Bl. The Q. Knight at his Q. 2d sq.

Wh. The Q. Pawn one sq.

---

by his having thus played his king's knight. You have still another advantage, by losing your king's bishop's pawn for his king's pawn, which is, when you do castle with your king's rook, the same rook finds itself immediately free and fit for action. This will be seen by the first back game.

(*b*) If he refuses taking your pawn, leave it in the same place exposed, except he should castle with his king's rook, in such case without any hesitation, or the interval of a single move, push it forwards in order to attack his king with all the pawns of your right wing. The effect of it will be learned by the second back game. See also Rule A. 3.

(*c*) If he takes your knight, take his bishop with your pawn, which being joined to his comrades increases the strength of your game.

8.

Bl. The K. Bishop at his Q. Kt. 3d sq.

Wh. The K. Bishop at his Q. 3d sq. (*d*)

9.

Bl. The Queen at her K. 2d sq.

Wh. The same.

10.

Bl. The King castles with his Rook (*e*) ☜

Wh. The Q. Knight at his Q. 2d sq.

11.

Bl. The K. Knight at his R. 4th sq. (*f*)

Wh. The Queen at her K. 3d sq.

12.

Bl. The K. Knight takes the Q. Bishop.(*g*)

(*d*) This is the best square your king's bishop can chuse, except his queen's bishop's 4th; particularly when you have the attack, and it be out of your adversary's power to hinder that bishop from playing on his king's bishop's pawn.

(*e*) If he had castled on his queen's side, it would have been your play to castle on your king's side, in order to attack him more commodiously with your pawns, on the left. This attack at your left will be seen by the third back game, and see Rule C. 2.

(*f*) To make room for his king's bishop's pawn, with a design to advance it two squares, to break the chain of your pawns.

(*g*) If, instead of this, he had pushed his king's bi-

Wh. The Queen takes the Knight.

13.

Bl. The Q. Bishop takes the Knight. (*h*)

Wh. The Pawn takes the Bishop.

14.

Bl. The K. B. Pawn 2 sq.

Wh. The Queen at her K. Kt. 3d sq.

15.

Bl. The K. B. Pawn takes the Pawn.

Wh. The K. B. Pawn takes it.

16.

Bl. The K. Rook at its K. B. 3d sq. (*i*)

Wh. The K. R. Pawn 2 sq. (*k*)

---

shop's pawn, you must then have attacked his queen with your queen's bishop, and pushed your king's rook's pawn the next move upon his bishop, to force him to take your knight; then your best way, as before, would be then to take his bishop with your pawn, in order the better to support your king's pawn, and replace it in case it be taken.

(*h*) If he did not take your knight his bishop would remain imprisoned by your pawns, or he would lose at least three moves to get him free, which are sufficient to spoil his game.

(*i*) He plays this rook, either to double it or to remove your queen.

(*k*) To give your queen more room, which being attacked can retire behind this pawn, and then remain

17.

Bl. The Q. Rook at its K. B. sq.
Wh. The King castles with his Q. Rook.

18.

Bl. The Q. B. Pawn 2 sq.
Wh. The K. Pawn one sq. (*l*)

---

battering upon her adversary's king's rook's pawn. The pawn advancing afterwards will become dangerous to your adversary's king.

(*l*) In order to comprehend this move, see Rule G. 3. and then observe, that your king's pawn not being in the line with his comrades, your adversary has pushed his queen's bishop's pawn two squares; first, to engage you to push that of your queen forwards, according to Rule A. 6, which, if you did, would be stopped by that of his queen's; and thus leaving behind that of your king, would render it useless: secondly, to hinder your king's bishop battering upon his king's rook's pawn; therefore it is best to push your king's pawn upon his rook, and sacrifice it; because then your adversary by taking it, and he cannot well do otherwise, opens a free passage to your queen's pawn, which you are to advance immediately, and sustain in case of need with your other pawns, in order to make a queen with it, or draw some other considerable advantage from it. It is true, that his queen's pawn (now become his king's) appears to have the same advantage of having no opposition from your pawns to make a queen; however, the difference is great, because his pawn being entirely se-

N

19.

Bl. The Q. Pawn takes the Pawn.
Wh. The Q. Pawn one sq.

20.

Bl. The Bishop at his Q. B. 2d sq.
Wh. The Knight at his K. 4th sq. (*m*)

21.

Bl. The K. Rook at the wh. K. B. 3d sq.
Wh. The Queen at her K. Kt. 2d sq.

22

Bl. The Queen at her K. B. 2d sq. (*n*)
Wh. The Knight at the bl. K. Kt. 4th sq.

---

parated from his comrades, will always be in danger of being captured in his road from a multitude of your pieces all at war against it. To know well how to make use of these moves at proper times and vary from established rules, one must be already a good player.

(*m*) It was necessary to play that knight in order to stop his king's pawn; the more so, because this very pawn, in its present situation, stops the passage of his own bishop, and even of his knight.

(*n*) In order afterwards to give you check, if he had played his king's rook's pawn to hinder the attack of your knight, you must have attacked his bishop and his queen with your queen's pawn; and in this case he would have been forced to take your pawn, and you should have taken his bishop with your knight, which he could not have taken with his queen, because she would have been lost by your bishop checking his king, leaving her in check by your rook.

23.

Bl. The Queen gives *check.*

Wh. The King at his Q. Kt. sq.

24.

Bl. The Rook takes the Bishop. (*o*)

Wh. The Rook takes the Rook.

25.

Bl. The Queen at her K. B. 4th sq.

Wh. The Queen at her K. 4th sq. (*p*)

26.

Bl. The Queen takes the Queen.

Wh. The Knight takes the Queen.

27.

Bl. The Rook at the wh. K. B. 4th sq.

Wh The Knight at the bl. K. Kt. 4th sq.

28.

Bl. The Q. B. Pawn one sq.

Wh. The Q. Rook at her K. Kt. 3d sq.

(*o*) First, to save his king's rook's pawn, and because your bishop proves incommodious to him; and secondly, to put his queen upon the rook that covers your king.

(*p*) Having a rook against a bishop at the end of a party, it is your advantage to change queens, particularly as his is at present troublesome to you where he has just played her; you force him to change, if he will save his being check-mated.

29.

Bl. The Knight at his Q. B. 4th sq.
Wh. The Knight at the bl. K. 3d sq.

30.

Bl. The Knight takes the Knight.
Wh. The Pawn takes the Knight.

31.

Bl. The Rook at his K. B. 3d sq.
Wh. The K. Rook at its Q. sq. (*q*)

32.

Bl. The Rook takes the Pawn.
Wh. The K. Rook at the bl. Q. 2d sq. and
must win the game. (*r*)

FIRST BACK GAME.

3.

Bl. The Q. Pawn 2 sq.
Wh. The K. B. Pawn 2 sq.

4.

Bl. The Q. Pawn takes the Pawn. (*a*)
Wh. The K. B. Pawn takes the Pawn.

(*q*) See Rule C. 18.

(*r*) He could not hinder you from doubling your rooks, unless he had sacrificed his bishop, or let you make a queen with your pawn.

(*a*) If he had taken your king's bishop's pawn instead of this, you must have pushed your king's pawn upon his knight, and afterwards taken his pawn with your queen's bishop.

5.

Bl. The K. Knight at the wh. K. Kt. 4th sq.

Wh. The Q. Pawn one sq.

6.

Bl. The K. B. Pawn 2 sq.

Wh. The K. Bishop at his Q. B. 4th sq.

7.

Bl. The Q. B. Pawn 2 sq.

Wh. The Q. B. Pawn one sq.

8.

Bl. The Q. Knight at his B. 3d sq.

Wh. The K. Knight at his K. 2d sq.

9.

Bl. The K. R. Pawn 2 sq. (*b*)

Wh. The K. R. Pawn one sq.

10.

Bl. The K. Knight at his R. 3d sq.

Wh. The King castles.

11.

Bl. The Q. Knight at his R. 4th sq.

Wh. The K. Bishop gives *check.*

(*b*) He pushes his pawn two squares to avoid having a double pawn upon his king's rook's line, which by pushing your king's rook's pawn upon his knight, he could not possibly avoid; and your taking it afterwards with your queen's bishop, would have given him a very bad game.

12.

Bl. The Q. Bishop covers the check.
Wh. The Bishop takes the Bishop.

13.

Bl. The Queen takes the Bishop.
Wh. The Q. Pawn one sq.

14.

Bl. The Q. B. Pawn one sq. (*c*)
Wh. The Q. Kt. Pawn 2 sq.

15.

Bl. The Q. B. Pawn takes it in passing.
Wh. The R. Pawn takes the Pawn.

16.

Bl. The Q. Kt. Pawn one sq.
Wh. The Q. Bishop at his K. 3d sq.

17.

Bl. The Bishop at his K. 2d sq.
Wh. The K. Knight at his K. B. 4th sq. (*d*)

(*c*) To cut off the communication of your pawns; but you avoid it by pushing your queen's knight's pawn upon his knight, which having no retreat, obliges your adversary to take the pawn by the way. This rejoins your pawns again, and makes them invincible.

(*d*) This knight seems to be of very little consequence; nevertheless it is he that gives the mortal blow, because he holds at present all your adversary's pieces in some measure locked up, till you have time to prepare the checkmate.

18.

Bl. The K. Knight at his own sq.
Wh. The K. Knight at the bl. K. Kt. 3d sq.

19.

Bl. The K. Rook at its 2d sq.
Wh. The K. Pawn one sq.

20.

Bl. The Queen at her Kt. 2d sq.
Wh. The Q. Pawn one sq.

21.

Bl. The K. Bishop at his 3d sq.
Wh. The K. Rook takes the Pawn.

22.

Bl. The King castles.
Wh. The K. Rook takes the Q. Knight.

23.

Bl. The Pawn takes the Rook.
Wh. The Q. Rook takes the Pawn.

24.

Bl. The Q. R. Pawn one sq.
Wh. The Rook gives *check*.

25.

Bl. The King at his Q. Kt. sq.
Wh. The Rook at the bl. Q. B. 2d sq.

26.

Bl. The Queen at her Kt. 4th sq.
Wh. The Q. Knight at his R. 3d sq.

27.

Bl. The Queen at her K. B. 4th sq.

Wh. The Q. Knight at her B. 4th sq.

28.

Bl. The Queen takes the Knight, knowing not to do better,

Wh. The Bishop gives *check.*

29.

Bl. The King at his Q. R. sq.

Wh. The Knight gives *checkmate.*

SECOND BACK GAME.

5.

Bl. The King castles.

Wh. The K. B. Pawn one sq.

6.

Bl. The Q. Pawn one sq.

Wh. The Queen at her K. B. 3d sq.

7.

Bl. The Q. Pawn takes the Pawn.

Wh. The Q. Pawn takes the Pawn.

8.

Bl. The Q. R. Pawn 2 sq.

Wh. The K. Kt. Pawn 2 sq.

9.

Bl. The Queen at her 3d sq.

Wh. The K. Kt. Pawn one sq.

10.

Bl. The K. Knight at his K. sq.

Wh. The K. Bishop at his Q. B. 4th sq.

11.

Bl. The Q. B. Pawn one sq.

Wh. The Queen at the bl. K. R. 4th sq.

12.

Bl. The Q. Kt. Pawn 2 sq.

Wh. The K. Kt. Pawn one sq.

13.

Bl. The K. R. Pawn one sq.

Wh. The K. Bishop takes the K. B. Pawn, and gives *check.*

14.

Bl. The King at his R. sq.

Wh. The Q. Bishop takes the K. R. Pawn.

15.

Bl. The K. Knight at his B. 3d sq.

Wh. The Queen at her K. R. 4th sq. and wins the game on removing the bishop.

THIRD BACK GAME,

10.

Bl. The King castles on his Queen's side.

Wh. The King castles on his own side.

11.

Bl. The K. R. Pawn one sq.

Wh. The Q. Knight at his Q. 2d sq.

12.

Bl. The K. Kt. Pawn 2 sq.
Wh. The Q. Bishop at his K. 3d sq.

13.

Bl. The Q. Rook at its K. Kt. sq.
Wh. The Q. Kt. Pawn 2 sq.

14.

Bl. The K. R. Pawn one sq.
Wh. The Q. R. Pawn 2 sq. (*a*)

15.

Bl. The Bishop takes the Knight.
Wh. The Queen takes the Bishop.

16.

Bl. The K. Kt. Pawn one sq.
Wh. The Queen at her K. 2d sq.

17.

Bl. The Q. B. Pawn one sq.
Wh. The Q. R. Pawn one sq.

18.

Bl. The Bishop at his Q. B. 2d sq.
Wh. The Q. B. Pawn one sq.

(*a*) It would have been very ill played to have pushed your king's rook's pawn upon his bishop, because he would have got the attack upon you by taking your knight with his bishop, and an opening upon your king by pushing his king's knight's pawn: this might have lost you the game. See Rule G. 16.

19.

Bl. The K. R. Pawn one sq.

Wh. The K. R. at its Q. Kt. sq.

20.

Bl. The K. Rook at its 4th sq.

Wh. The Q. Bishop Pawn one sq.

21.

Bl. The Q. Pawn one sq.

Wh. The K. Pawn one sq.

22.

Bl. The K. Kt. at his K. sq.

Wh. The Q. Kt. Pawn one sq.

23.

Bl. The Q. B. Pawn takes the Pawn.

Wh. The K. Rook takes the Pawn.

24.

Bl. The Q. R. Pawn one sq.

Wh. The K. Rook at his Q. Kt. 4th sq.

25.

Bl. The K. B. Pawn one sq.

Wh. The K. Bishop takes the Q. R. Pawn.

26.

Bl. The Pawn takes the Bishop.

Wh. The Queen takes the Pawn, and *checks.*

27.

Bl. The King at his Q. sq.

Wh. The Queen gives *check.*

28.

Bl. The Knight covers the *check*.

Wh. The Q. R. Pawn one sq.

29.

Bl. The King at his Queen's 2d sq.

Wh. The Queen takes the Q. Pawn and *checks*.

30.

Bl. The King at his B. sq.

Wh. The Q. R. Pawn one sq. and, by different obvious ways, the wh. wins the game.

FOURTH PARTY,

TWO BACK GAMES.

———

1.

Bl. THE K. Pawn 2 sq.
Wh. The same.

2.

Bl. The Q. B. Pawn one sq. (*a*)
Wh. The Q. Pawn 2 sq.

3.

Bl. The Pawn takes the Pawn.
Wh. The Queen takes the Pawn.

4.

Bl. The Q. Pawn one sq. (*b*)
Wh. The K. B. Pawn 2 sq.

———

(*a*) This (unless one is sure of playing with a bungler) is ill played, because the move is lost by the adversary pushing the queen's pawn two squares: the attack going on the other side, very probably the game will also; for, when once the move is lost, it is very difficult to regain it with good players. 'T is true, if you were to neglect pushing your queen's pawn he would lock up all your game with his pawns.

(*b*) If he had played his king's knight at his king's second square you must have pushed your king's pawn

5.

Bl. The K. B. Pawn 2 sq. (*c*)

Wh. The K. Pawn one sq. (*d*)

6.

Bl. The Q. Pawn one sq. (*e*)

Wh. The Queen at her K. B. 2d sq.

7.

Bl. The Q. Bishop at his K. 3d sq. ,

Wh. The K. Knight at his B. 3d sq.

8.

Bl. The Q. Knight at his Q. 2d sq.

---

forwards, and sustained it with your king's bishop's pawn.

(*c*) If he had played his queen's bishop at his king's third square, you must have played your king's bishop at his queen's third square, and the situation of the game would have been in this case exactly as it is at the sixth move of the second party (*vide* p. 178). But if he had attacked your queen with his queen's bishop's pawn, he would have lost the game; because the pawn that formed the vanguard on his queen's side is left behind (*vide* (*l*) the eighteenth move of the Third Party p. 193). A back game will better clear this situation, and the progress of it.

(*d*) See Rule E. 2.

(*e*) If he had taken your king's pawn, you must have taken his queen, and afterwards his pawn : thus hindering him from castling, you preserve the attack upon him. But had he played his queen at her bishop's second square, you would have played according to the second back game.

Wh. The K. Knight at his Q. 4th sq.

9.

Bl. The K. Bishop at his Q. B. 4th sq.

Wh. The Q. B. Pawn one sq.

10.

Bl. The Queen at her Kt. 3d sq.

Wh. The Q. Bishop at his K. 3d sq.

11.

Bl. The K. Bishop takes the Knight.

Wh. The Pawn takes the Bishop. *(f)*

12.

Bl. The K. Knight at his K. 2d sq.

Wh. The K. Bishop at his Q. 3d sq.

13.

Bl. The King castles with his Rook.

Wh. The K. R. Pawn one sq.

14.

Bl. The Queen at her B. 2d sq. *(g)*

Wh. The K. Kt. Pawn 2 sq.

15.

Bl. The K. Kt. Pawn one sq.

Wh. The same. *(h)*

(*f*) See Rule A 9.

(*g*) Being now of no use in that place, he removes her to make room for his pawns.

(*h*) The pushing of this Pawn obstructs his game the more: your king's rook's pawn who is to follow it will

16.

Bl. The Q. Kt. Pawn one sq.
Wh. The Q. Knight at his B. 3d sq.

17.

Bl. The Q. B. Pawn one sq.
Wh. The King castles on his Q. side. (*i*)

18.

Bl. The Q. B. Pawn takes the Pawn.
Wh. The Q. Bishop takes the Pawn.

19.

Bl. The Q. Knight at his Q. B. 4th sq.
Wh. The K. R. Pawn one sq. (*k*)

20.

Bl. The Knight takes the K. Bishop.
Wh. The Rook takes the Knight.

---

be always in a condition to make an opening upon his king as soon as your pieces are all ready to form your attack; it is what he can no longer avoid.

(*i*) You castle on this side to have a freer attack on your right wing; if instead of castling you had taken the pawn offered to you, you would have played very ill, because his queen's pawn would have united that of his queen's bishop in a front line, and would have proved very incommodious to all your pieces: besides, pawns are seldom offered without a view of some considerable advantage.

(*k*) Had you taken his knight with your queen's bishop, you had fallen into that very error which you strove to avoid by not taking the pawn offered to you before.

21.

Bl. The Q. Bishop at his K. B. 2d sq. (*l*)

Wh. The K. R. Pawn one sq.

22.

Bl. The Q. Kt. Pawn one sq. (*m*)

Wh. The Q. Rook at its K. R. 3d sq.

23.

Bl. The Q. Kt. Pawn one sq.

Wh. The K. Pawn one sq.

24.

Bl. The Bishop at his K. sq. (*n*)

Wh. The K. R. Pawn takes the Pawn.

25.

Bl. The Bishop takes the Pawn.

Wh. The Rook takes the K. R. Pawn.

26.

Bl. The Bishop takes the Rook.

Wh. The K. Rook takes the Bishop.

27.

Bl. The King takes the Rook.

(*l*) To replace his king's knight's pawn in case it be taken.

(*m*) To attack the knight that covers your king, knowing not to do better, for had he taken your pawn, he would have lost the game equally.

(*n*) If he takes the pawn in lieu of retiring his bishop, he loses the game also.

o

Wh. The Queen *checks* at her K. R. 4th sq.

28.

Bl. King at his Kt. place, having no other.

Wh. The Queen gives *checkmate.* (*o*)

FIRST BACK GAME.

5.

Bl. The Q. B. Pawn one sq.

Wh. The K. Bishop gives *check.*

6.

Bl. The Bishop covers the Check.

Wh. The Bishop takes the Bishop.

7.

Bl. The Queen takes the Bishop.

Wh. The Queen at her 3d sq.

8.

Bl. The Q. Knight at his Bishop's 3d sq.

Wh. The Q. B. Pawn 2 sq.

9.

Bl. The Q. Knight at the wh. Q. Kt. 4th sq.

Wh. The Queen at her K. 2d sq.

10.

Bl. The K. Bishop at his K. 2d sq.

Wh. The Q. Knight at his B. 3d sq.

(*o*) See Rule C. 19.

11.

Bl The K. Bishop at his 3d sq.

Wh. The Q. Knight at the bl. Q. 4th sq.

12.

Bl. The Q. Knight takes the Knight. (*a*)

Wh. The K. Pawn takes the Knight. (*b*)

13.

Bl. The Knight at his K. 2d sq.

Wh. The K. Knight at his B. 3d sq.

14.

Bl. The King castles with his Rook.

Wh. The Queen at her 3d sq.

15.

Bl. The K. Rook at its K. sq.

Wh. The King at his B. 2d sq. (*c*)

16.

Bl. The Knight at his K. B. 4th sq.

(*a*) By this change he avoids his queen's pawn being attacked by your rooks; nevertheless, your king's pawn will win the game in spite of all he can do.

(*b*) Had you taken with your queen's bishop's pawn, he would have had it in his power to separate your pawns by pushing his king's bishop's pawn upon your king's pawn.

(*c*) If you had castled on your queen's side, your adversary's bishop would have been very incommodious to you, having his line quite open. See Rules B. 3, and G. 15.

Wh. The K. R. Pawn 2 sq.

17.

Bl. The Knight at the wh. Q. 4th sq.

Wh. The Q. Bishop at his K. 3d sq.

18.

Bl. The Knight takes the Knight.

Wh. The King takes the Knight.

19.

Bl. The Bishop takes the Q. Kt. Pawn.

Wh. The Q. Rook at his Kt. 2d sq.

20.

Bl. The Bishop retires to his 3d sq.

Wh. The K. Kt. Pawn 2 sq.

21.

Bl. The K. Kt. Pawn one sq.

Wh. The same.

22.

Bl. The Bishop at his K. Kt. 2d sq.

Wh. The K. R. Pawn one sq.

23.

Bl. The K. Rook at its K. 2d sq.

Wh. The K. Rook at its 4th sq.

24.

Bl. The Q. Rook at its K. sq.

Wh. The Bishop at its Q. 2d sq.

25.

Bl. The K. Rook at the wh. K. 4th sq.

Wh. The R. Pawn takes the Pawn.

26.

Bl. The R. Pawn takes the Pawn.

Wh. The Q. Rook at her K. R. sq.

27.

Bl. The Q. Kt. Pawn 2 sq.

Wh. The Bishop at his Q. B. 3d sq.

28.

Bl. The Rook gives *check.*

Wh. The King at his B. 2d sq.

29.

Bl. The Rook takes the Queen.

Wh. The Rook gives *checkmate* at the black
K. R. sq. *

SECOND BACK GAME.

6.

Bl. The Queen at her B. 2d sq.

Wh. The K. Bishop at his Q. B. 4th sq.

7.

Bl. The Q. Pawn takes the Pawn.

Wh. The Pawn takes the Pawn.

8.

Bl. The Q. B. Pawn one sq.

---

* The conclusion of this game does not appear quite
correct, as it might be easily procrastinated, *at least,*
by several exchanges that obviously present themselves
after the 27th. move. *Ed.*

Wh. The Queen at the bl. Q. 4th sq.

9.

Bl. The Q. Knight at his B. 3d sq.

Wh. The K. Knight at his B. 3d sq.

10.

Bl. The Q. Knight at the wh. Q. Kt. 4th sq.

Wh. The Queen at her own sq.

11.

Bl. The Q. R. Pawn one sq.

Wh. The Q. R. Pawn 2 sq.

12.

Bl. The K. Knight at his K. 2d sq.

Wh. The King castles.

13.

Bl. The K. Kt. Pawn one sq.

Wh. The Q. Bishop at the bl. K. Kt. 4th sq.

14.

Bl. The K. Bishop at his Kt. 2d sq.

Wh. The Q. Bishop at the bl. K. B. 3d sq.

15.

Bl. The K. Knight at his own sq.

Wh. The Q. Bishop takes the Bishop.

16.

Bl. The Queen takes the Bishop.

Wh. The K. Knight at the bl. K. Kt 4th sq.

17.

Bl. The K. Knight at his R. 3d sq.

Wh. The Q. Knight at his B. 3d sq.

18.

Bl. The Q. Knight at his B. 3d sq.
Wh. The Queen at the bl. Q. 4th sq.

19.

Bl. The Q. Knight at his K. 2d sq.
Wh. The Queen at the bl. Q. 3d sq.

20.

Bl. The Q. Bishop at his Q. 2d sq.
Wh. The K. Pawn one sq.

21.

Bl. The Q. Bishop at his 3d sq.
Wh. The Q. Rook at its Q. sq.

22.

Bl. The K. Knight at the wh. K. Kt. 4th sq.
Wh. The Queen *checks* at the bl. Q. 2d sq.

23.

Bl. The Bishop takes the Queen.
Wh. The Pawn takes the Bishop, and *checks*.

24.

Bl. The King at his Q. sq.
Wh. The Knight gives Checkmate at the bl. K. 3d sq. *

---

* Though this back game may be played several different ways, the black will always lose the game, if you take care to suffer no obstruction to your king's bishop.

Another way of exemplifying the danger of playing the Q. B. Pawn the 2d move.

1.

Bl. The K. Pawn 2 sq.

Wh. The same.

2.

Bl. The Q. B. Pawn one sq.

Wh. The Q. Pawn 2 sq.

3.

Bl. The Pawn takes the Pawn.

Wh. The Queen takes the Pawn.

4.

Bl. The Q. Pawn 2 sq.

Wh. The Pawn takes the Pawn.

5.

Bl. The Pawn takes the Pawn.

Wh: The Q. B. Pawn 2 sq.

6.

Bl. The Q. Bishop at his K. 3d sq.

Wh. The Pawn takes the Pawn.

7.

Bl. The Queen takes the Pawn.

Wh. The Queen takes the Queen.

8.

Bl. The Bishop takes the Queen.

Wh. The Q. Knight at his B. 3d sq.

(*a*) Without going any further, I leave to consider whether the black has made any thing of his attack, though he played the very best moves.

217

FIRST GAMBIT,

WITH

SIX BACK GAMES.

1.

Bl. The K. Pawn 2 sq. (*a*)
Wh. The same.

2.

Wh. The K. B. Pawn 2 sq.
Bl. The K. Pawn takes it.

3.

Wh. The K. Knight at his B. 3d sq.
Bl. The K. Kt. Pawn 2 sq.

4.

Wh. The K. Bishop at his Q. B. 4th (*b*)
Bl. The K. Bishop at his Kt. 2d sq.

(*a*) See Rule C. 21.

(*b*) If you had pushed your king's rook's pawn two steps, before you had played this bishop, your adversary would have abandoned the gambit's pawn, and by so doing would have gained the attack upon you, with a better situation of game. This will be demonstrated by my first back-game, beginning at the fourth move.

5.

Wh. The K. R. Pawn 2 sq. (*c*)
Bl. The K. R. Pawn one sq. ☞

6.

Wh. The Q. Pawn 2 sq.
Bl. The Q. Pawn one sq. ☞

7.

Wh. The Q. B. Pawn one sq.
Bl. The same. ☞

8.

Wh. The Queen at her Kt. 3d sq.
Bl. The Queen at her K. second sq.

9.

Wh. The King castles.
Bl. The Q. Kt. Pawn 2 sq. (*d*) ☞

10.

Wh. The K. Bishop at his Q. 3d sq.
Bl. The Q. R. Pawn one sq.

11.

Wh. The Q. R. Pawn 2 sq.
Bl. The Q. Bishop at his Q. Kt. 2d sq.

(*c*) In order to make him advance his king's rook's pawn, by which move his king's knight becomes a prisoner.

(*d*) As he has broken your attack on the king's side by this move, you must remove it to the queen's side as follows, and you will equally win the game.

12.

Wh. The Q. Knight at his R. 3d sq.

Bl. The Q. Knight at his Q. 2d sq.

13.

Wh. The Q. Bishop at his Q. 2d sq.

Bl. The Queen at her K. B. 3d sq.

14.

Wh. The Q. R. Pawn takes the Pawn.

Bl. The Q. R. Pawn takes it.

15.

Wh. The Q. Knight takes the Pawn.

Bl. The Pawn takes the Knight.

16.

Wh. The Queen takes the Pawn.

Bl. The Rook at its Kt. sq.

17.

Wh. The K. R. Pawn takes the Pawn.

Bl. The Pawn takes it.

18.

Wh. The Queen takes the K. Kt. Pawn.

Bl. The Queen takes the Queen.

19.

Wh. The Knight takes the Queen.

Bl. The K. Knight at his R. 3d sq.

20.

Wh. The Q. Bishop takes the Pawn.

Bl. The K. Bishop at his square.

21.

Wh. The Q. Kt. Pawn 2 sq. (*e*)

FIRST BACK GAME.

4.
Wh. The K. R. Pawn 2 sq.
Bl. The K. Kt. Pawn one sq.

5.
Wh. The K. Knight at the bl. K. 4th sq.
Bl. The K. R. Pawn 2 sq.

6.
Wh. The K. Bishop at his Q. B. 4th sq.
Bl. The K. Rook at its 2d sq.

7.
Wh. The Q. Pawn 2 sq.
Bl. The Q. Pawn one sq.

8.
Wh. The K. Knight at his Q. 3d sq.
Bl. The Queen at her K. 2d sq.

9.
Wh. The Q. Knight at his B. 3d sq.
Bl. The K. Knight at his B. 3d. sq.

(*e*) The white must win the game, not only by the strength of the pawns, but by the extreme bad situation of the black, he having not one good or saving move.

10.

Wh. The Queen at her K. 2d. sq.

Bl. The K. Pawn one sq.

11.

Wh. The K. Kt. Pawn takes the Pawn.

Bl. The same.

12.

Wh. The Queen takes the Pawn.

Bl. The Q. Bishop at the wh. K. Kt. 4th.

13.

Wh. The Queen at her K. 3d sq.

Bl. The K. Bishop at his R. 3d. sq.

14.

Wh. The K. Knight at his K. B. 4th sq.

Bl. The Q. B. Pawn one sq.

15.

Wh. The Q. Bishop at his Q. 2d sq. (*a*)

Bl. The K. Bishop takes the Knight.

16.

Wh. The Queen takes the Bishop.

Bl. The Q. Pawn one sq.

17.

Wh. The K. Bishop at his Q. 3d sq.

Bl. The K. Knight takes the K. Pawn.

(*a*) If you had pushed your king's pawn, the pawn would equally have been lost by his attacking it with his queen's knight.

18.
Wh. The Bishop, or Knight, takes the Knight
Bl. The K. B. Pawn 2 sq. *(b)*

SECOND BACK GAME.

4.
Wh. The K. Bishop at his Q. B. 4th sq.
Bl. The K. Kt. Pawn one sq.

5.
Wh. The K. Knight at the bl. K. 4th sq.
Bl. The Queen gives *check.*

6.
Wh. The King at his Bishop's sq.
Bl. The K. Knight at his R. 3d sq.

7.
Wh. The Q. Pawn 2 sq.
Bl. The Q. Pawn one sq.

8.
Wh. The K. Knight at his Q. 3d sq.
Bl. The K. Pawn one sq.

(*b*) The same pawn afterwards takes his knight, and must infallibly win the game. Those who have made a little advantage by the lessons given in the first four parties, have no occasion for any instruction to finish this, and to win it. This last pawn, now become royal, sustained as it is, and at the head of his comrades, is worth one of the best pieces. So it is needless to go further with this first back game.

9.

Wh. The K. Kt. Pawn one sq.
Bl. The Queen gives *check.*

10.

Wh. The King at his B. 2d sq.
Bl. The Queen gives *check..*

11.

Wh. The King at his 3d sq.
Bl. The K. Knight at his place (*a*)

12.

Wh. The K. Knight at his K. B. 4th sq.
Bl. The K. Bishop at his R. 3d sq.

13.

Wh. The K. Bishop at his home.
Bl. The Queen takes the Rook.

14.

Wh. The K. Bishop gives *check,* and takes
the Queen afterwards. (*b*)

(*a*) To make room for his king's bishop, in order to attack your king with it, being his best move in the present situation.

(*b*) I have no need to go further in this game, since it is evident that the white must win.

THIRD BACK GAME.

5.

Wh. The K. R. Pawn 2 sq.

Bl. The K. Kt. Pawn one sq.

6.

Wh. The K. Knight at the bl. K. Kt. 4th sq.

Bl. The K. Knight at his R. 3d sq.

7.

Wh. The Q. Pawn 2 sq.

Bl. The K. B. Pawn one sq.

8.

Wh. The Q. Bishop takes the Pawn.

Bl. The Q. Pawn one sq.

9.

Wh. The Q. B. Pawn one sq.

Bl. The Pawn takes the Knight. (*a*)

10.

Wh. The Pawn takes the Pawn.

Bl. The K. Knight at his home.

11.

Wh. The Queen at her Kt. 3d sq.

Bl. The Queen at her K. 2d sq.

12.

Wh. The Q. Knight at his Q. 2d sq.

(*a*) If he had taken your knight before he had made room for his queen by pushing her pawn, you must have taken his with your bishop.

Bl. The Queen at her K. B. sq.

13.

Wh. The King castles with his Rook.

Bl. Loses the game (*b*)

FOURTH BACK GAME.

6.

Wh. The Q. Pawn 2 sq.

Bl. The Q. B. Pawn one sq. (*a*)

7.

Wh. The K. Pawn one sq.

Bl. The Q. Kt. Pawn 2 sq.

8.

Wh. The Bishop at his Q. Kt. 3d sq.

Bl. The Q. R. Pawn 2 sq.

9.

Wh. The Q. R. Pawn 2 sq.

Bl. The Q. Kt. Pawn one sq.

(*b*) If he plays his queen to avoid the discovering your rook upon her, he loses his knight ; and if he plays his knight he loses his queen. It is visible he loses the game every way.

(*a*) To attack afterwards your king's bishop with his queen's pawn, which you prevent by pushing your king's pawn.

P

10.

Wh. The Q. Knight at his Q. 2d. sq. (*b*)

Bl. The Q. Bishop at his R. 3d sq.

11.

Wh. The Q. Knight at his K. 4th sq.

Bl. The Queen at her Kt. 3d sq. or any
where else, as he loses the game.

12.

Wh. The Knight *checks* at the bl. Q. 3d sq.

———

FIFTH BACK GAME.

7.

Wh. The Q. B. Pawn one sq.

Bl. The Q. Bishop at the wh. K. Kt. 4th sq.

8.

Wh. The Queen at her Kt. 3d sq.

Bl. The Q. Bishop at his K. R. 4th sq. (*a*)

9.

Wh. The K. R. Pawn takes the Pawn.

Bl. The R. Pawn takes the Pawn.

———

(*b*) This knight, which appeared insignificant in his
situation, is now the very piece that will win the game,
without possibility of the adversary hindering it: therefore observe Rule A. 5.

(*a*) If he had sustained his king's bishop's pawn with
his queen, you had then taken his queen's knight's pawn,
and afterwards his rook.

10.

Wh. The K. Rook takes the Bishop.

Bl. The Rook takes the Rook.

11.

Wh. The K. Bishop takes the Pawn *(b)*

SIXTH BACK GAME.

9.

Wh. The King castles.

Bl. The Q. Knight at his Q. 2d sq.

10.

Wh. The K. R. Pawn takes the Pawn.

Bl. The Pawn takes it.

11.

Wh. The K. Knight takes the Pawn.

Bl. The Queen takes the Knight.

12.

Wh. K. Bishop takes the Pawn, and *checks*

Bl. The King at his B. sq.

13.

Wh. The Q. Bishop takes the Pawn.

Bl. The Queen at the wh. K. R. 4th sq.

(*b*) Giving check to both king and rook, he wins a piece, and soon afterwards the game.

P 2

14.

Wh. Q. Bishop takes the Pawn, and *checks*.

Bl. The K. Knight covers the Check.

15.

Wh. The K. Bishop at the bl. K. Kt. 3d sq.
and gives *check* by Discovery.

Bl. Any thing, losing the Game.

SECOND GAMBIT,

WITH

FOUR BACK GAMES.

1.

Wh. THE K. Pawn 2 sq.
Bl. The same.

2.

Wh. The K. B. Pawn 2 sq.
Bl. The Pawn takes the Pawn.

3.

Wh. The K. Bishop at his Q. B. 4th sq.
Bl. The Queen gives *check.*

4.

Wh. The King at his B. sq.
Bl. The K. Kt. Pawn 2 sq. ☞

5.

Wh. The K. Knight at his B. 3d sq.
Bl. The Queen at her K. R. 4th sq. (*a*)

(*a*) He may play his queen in three different places, but all very bad, except this: because, if he retires her at the rook's third square, you have only to attack his

6.
Wh. The Q. Pawn 2 sq.
Bl. The Q. Pawn one sq.

7.
Wh. The Q. B. Pawn one sq. (*b*)
Bl. Q. Bishop at the wh. K. Kt. 4th sq.

8.
Wh. The King at his B. 2d sq.
Bl. The K. Knight at his K. B. 3d sq.

9.
Wh. The Queen at her K. 2d sq.
Bl. The Q. Knight at his Q. 2d sq. ☞

10.
Wh. The K. R. Pawn 2 sq.
Bl. The Bishop takes the Knight.

11.
Wh. The Queen takes the Bishop.
Bl. The Queen takes the Queen. ☞

---

king's bishop's pawn with your knight, by playing it at your adversary's king's fourth square, and you will gain a rook by it; if he plays her at your king's knight's fourth square, you are to give him check, by taking his king's bishop's pawn with your bishop; and in case he takes your bishop, you will check his king and queen with your knight, and consequently win the game.

(*b*) See Rule C. 13.

12.

Wh. The King takes the Queen *(c)*

Bl. The K. Kt. Pawn gives *check.*

13.

Wh. The King takes the K. Pawn.

Bl. K. Bishop *checks* at the Rook's 3d sq.

14.

Wh. The King at the bl. K. Bishop 4th sq.

Bl. The K. Bishop takes the Q. Bishop.

15.

Wh. The Rook takes the Bishop.

Bl. The K. R. Pawn 2 sq.

16.

Wh. The Knight at his Q. 2d sq.

Bl. The King at his 2d sq.

17.

Wh. The K. Rook at its K. B. sq.

Bl. The Q. B. Pawn one sq.

(c) I have given it as a general rule, to unite your king's and king's bishop's pawn together: but you will here find an objection for two good reasons. First, if you take with your king, you gain a pawn, your adversary being no more able to hinder it; and secondly, the king having but little to fear when the queens are out of the way, you must get him into action, in order that he may be useful.

232

PHILIDOR'S ANALYSIS.PHILIDOR'S ANALYSIS.
PHILIDOR'S ANALYSIS.

18.## 18.

Wh. The Q. Rook at its K. sq.*Wh.* The Q. Rook at its K. sq.
Bl. The Q. Kt. Pawn 2 sq.

19.

Wh. The Bishop at his Q. Kt. 3d sq.
Bl. The Q. R. Pawn 2 sq.

20.

Wh. The K. Pawn one sq.
Bl. The Pawn takes the Pawn.

21.

Wh. The Q. Pawn takes the Pawn.
Bl. The K. Knight at his Q. 4th sq.

22.

Wh. The Knight at his K. 4th sq. (*d*)
Bl. The Q. Knight at his 3d sq.

23.

Wh. The Knight at the bl. K. B. 3d sq.
Bl. The Q. Rook at its Q. sq. (*e*)

(*d*) If you had taken his knight with your bishop, it would have been ill played, because he would have taken it with his pawn, and this pawn would have stopped the progress of your knight. It was therefore necessary to advance your knight first, in order to have no useless pieces in your game.

(*e*) If he had taken your knight, you must have taken it with your pawn, and afterwards played your queen's rook at your king's second square, and attacked his king's bishop's pawn.

24.

Wh. The K. Pawn one sq.

Bl. The Q. Rook at its Q. 3d sq. (*f*)

25.

Wh. The Pawn takes the Pawn and *checks* with the Rook.

Bl. The King takes the Pawn.

26.

Wh. The King at the bl. K. Kt. 4th sq.

Bl. The King at his Kt. 2d sq. (*g*)

27.

Wh. Knight takes the K. R. Pawn and *checks*

Bl. The King at his R. 2d sq.

28.

Wh. The K. Rook gives *check.*

Bl. The King at his Kt. sq.

29.

Wh. The K. Rook at the bl. Q. Kt. 2d sq.

Bl. The Q. Rook at his Q. sq. (*h*)

(*f*) If he had taken your pawn, he had lost the game in a few moves, for having lost his queen's bishop's pawn.

(*g*) To avoid a check by discovery.

(*h*) If he plays his king instead of his rook, you give check at his queen's knight's square, and take the king's rook, which is enough to win; your having had your king fit for action, and serving you all the latter part of the game better than any other piece upon the board, wins you the party.

30.

Wh. The Rook takes the Q. Knight and wins.

FIRST BACK GAME.

4.

Wh. The King at his B. sq.

Bl. The K. Bishop at his Q. B. 4th sq.

5.

Wh. The Q. Pawn 2 sq.

Bl. The K. Bishop at his Q. Kt. 3d sq.

6.

Wh. The K. Knight at his B. 3d sq.

Bl. The Queen at the wh. K. Kt. 4th sq.

7.

Wh. The K. Bishop takes the K. B. Pawn
and *checks.*

Bl. The King at his B. sq. (*a*)

8.

Wh. The K. R. Pawn one sq.

Bl. The Queen at the wh. K. Kt. 3d sq.

9.

Wh. The Q. Knight at his B. 3d sq.

(*a*) If he takes, he loses his queen, by the knight checking both her and the king.

Bl. The King takes the Bishop (*b*)

10.

Wh. The Q. Knight at his K. 2d sq.

Bl. The Queen at her K. Kt. 3d sq. (*c*)

11.

Wh. The K. Knight *checks* both King and Queen, and wins the game.

SECOND BACK GAME.

4.

Wh. The King at his Bishop's sq.

Bl. The Q. Pawn one sq.

5.

Wh. The K. Knight at his B. 3d sq.

Bl. The Q. Bishop at the wh. K. Kt. 4th sq.

6.

Wh. The Q. Pawn 2 sq.

Bl. The K. Kt. Pawn 2 sq.

7.

Wh. The Q. Knight at his B. 3d sq.

Bl. The Queen at her K. Rook's 4th sq. (*a*)

(*b*) If he does not take the bishop, it will come to the same thing, his queen having no way left to save herself.

(*c*) Having no other place.

(*a*) If he takes your king's knight, instead of retiring

8.

Wh. The K. R. Pawn 2 sq.

Bl. The K. R. Pawn one sq. (*b*)

9.

Wh. The King at his B. 2d sq.

Bl. The Q. Bishop takes the K. Knight. (*c*)

10.

Wh. The Pawn takes the Bishop.

Bl. The Queen at her K. Kt. 3d sq.

11.

Wh. The R. Pawn takes the Pawn.

Bl. The Queen takes the Pawn.

12.

Wh. The Knight at his K. 2d sq.

Bl. The Q. Knight at his Q. 2d sq.

13.

Wh. The Knight takes the Pawn.

Bl. The Queen at her Home.

---

his queen, take him with your queen, and pushing afterwards your king's knight's pawn one step, the situation of your game will become very good.

(*b*) If he had play'd his king's bishop's pawn, you must have taken his knight with your king's bishop, and then playing your queen's knight at his queen's fourth, you would have had again a very good situation.

(*c*) If he had retired his queen, or play'd any other piece, you must have taken his king's knight's pawn with your rook's pawn : see Rule C. 17.

14.

Wh. The Q. B. Pawn one sq.
Bl. The Q. Knight at his 3d sq.

15.

Wh. The K. Bishop at his Q. 3d sq.
Bl. The Queen at her 2d sq.

16.

Wh. The Q. Bishop at his K. 3d sq.
Bl. The King castles.

17.

Wh. The Q. R. Pawn 2 sq.
Bl. The King at his Q. Kt. sq.

18.

Wh. The Q. R. Pawn one sq.
Bl. The Q. Knight at his B. sq.

19.

Wh. The Q. Kt. Pawn 2 sq.
Bl. The Q. B. Pawn one sq.

20.

Wh. The Q. Kt. Pawn one sq.
Bl. The Pawn takes the Pawn.

21.

Wh. The Q. R. Pawn one sq. (*d*)
Bl. The Q. Kt. Pawn one sq.

(*d*) To hinder him from sustaining his queen's bishop's pawn.

22.

Wh. The Queen at her Kt. 3d sq.

Bl. The K. Knight at his B. 3 sq.

23.

Wh. The K. Bishop takes the Pawn

Bl. The Queen at her B. 2d sq.

24.

Wh. The Q. Pawn one sq.

Bl. The K. Bishop at his Kt. 2d sq.

25.

Wh. The K. Bishop at the bl. Q. B. 3d sq.

Bl. The K. Knight at his Q. 2d sq.

26.

Wh. The Knight at his Queen's 3d sq.

Bl. The K. Knight at his King's 4th sq.

27.

Wh. The Knight takes the Knight.

Bl. The Bishop takes the Knight.

28.

Wh. The K. B. Pawn one sq.

Bl. The Bishop at his K. Kt. 2d sq.

29.

Wh. The Q. Bishop at his Q. 4th sq.

Bl. The Bishop takes the Bishop.

30.

Wh. The Pawn takes the Bishop.

Bl. The Queen at her K. 2d sq.

31.

Wh. The King at his B. 3d sq.

Bl. The Q. Rook at its K. Kt. sq,

32.

Wh. The Q. Rook at its B. sq.

Bl. The Q. Rook at its K. Kt. 3d sq.

33.

Wh. The Bishop at the bl. Q. Kt. 2d sq.

Bl. The K. Rook at its Kt. sq.

34.

Wh. The Rook takes the Knight.

Bl. The Rook takes the Rook.

35.

Wh. The Bishop takes the Rook.

Bl. The King takes the Bishop.

36.

Wh. The Rook gives *check.*

Bl. The King at his Q. Kt. sq.

37.

Wh. The Queen at her B. 4th sq.

Bl. The Queen at her 2d sq.

38.

Wh. The K. B. Pawn one sq. to hinder the Queen's *check.*

Bl. The Rook at its K. Kt. sq.

39.

Wh. The Queen at the bl. Q. B. 3d sq.

Bl. The Queen takes the Queen (*f*)

40.

Wh. The Pawn takes the Queen.

Bl. The King at his Q. B. 2d sq.

41.

Wh. The Q. Pawn one sq.

Bl. The K. R. Pawn one sq.

42.

Wh. The Rook at its K. R. sq.

Bl. The same.

43.

Wh. The Rook at its K. Kt. sq.

Bl. The Rook at its 2d sq.

44.

Wh. The Rook at the bl. K. Kt. sq.

Bl. The Q. Kt. Pawn one sq. (*g*)

45.

Wh. The Rook at the bl. Q. R. sq.

Bl. The King at his Q. Kt. 3d sq.

46.

Wh. The Rook gives *check.*

Bl. The King at his Q. B. 2d sq.

(*f*) If his queen retires, you give him check-mate, or take his queen by pushing only your king's pawn.

(*g*) If he had pushed his king's rook's pawn in order to make a queen, you will see by calculation that he is one move short.

47.

Wh. The Rook *checks* at the bl. Q. Kt. 2d sq.

Bl. The King at his Q. sq.

48.

Wh. The K. Pawn one sq.

Bl. The Pawn takes the Pawn.

49.

Wh. The Q. Pawn one sq.

Bl. The King at his Q. B. sq. (*h*)

50.

Wh. The Q. Pawn gives *check*.

Bl. The King at his Q. sq.

51.

Wh. The Rook *checks*, the Pawn makes a
Queen, and wins the Game. (*i*)

THIRD BACK GAME.

9.

Wh. The Queen at her K. 2d sq.

Bl. The Bishop takes the Knight.

(*h*) To avoid the rook's giving checkmate.

(*i*) In this second back game, in which it is very difficult for the white to attain his aim, it would have been impossible to succeed without the help of the king; because had he castled on his queen's side, being so distant, he would have proved an obstacle instead of a help : see Rule B. 3.

Q

10.

Wh. The Queen takes the Bishop.

Bl. The Queen takes the Queen (*a*)

11.

Wh. The Pawn takes the Queen.

Bl. The K. Bishop at his Kt. 2d sq.

12.

Wh. The K. R. Pawn 2. sq.

Bl. The K. R. Pawn one sq.

13.

Wh. The K. Rook at his Kt. sq.

Bl. The K. Knight at his R. 2d sq.

14.

Wh. Q. Bishop takes the Gambit's Pawn.

Bl. K. Bishop takes the Q. Pawn, and *checks.*

15.

Wh. The Pawn takes the Bishop.

Bl. The K. Kt. Pawn takes the Bishop.

16.

Wh. The K. Rook at the bl. K. Kt. 2d sq.

Bl. The Q. Knight at his B. 3d sq.

17.

Wh. The Q. Knight at his B. 3d sq.

(*a*) If he had not taken your queen, you must have pushed immediately your king's rook's pawn two squares to separate his pawns.

Bl. The Q. Knight takes the Pawn.

18.

Wh. The Bishop takes the Pawn and *checks.*
Bl. The King at his B. sq.

19.

Wh. The Q. Rook at his K. Kt. sq.
Bl. The Q. Knight at his B. 3d sq.

20.

Wh. The Bishop at his Q. Kt. 3d sq.
Bl. The Q. Rook at its Q. sq. (*b*)

21.

Wh. K. Rook *checks* at the bl. K. B. 2d sq.
Bl. The King at his home.

22.

Wh. The Q. Rook at the bl. K. Kt. 2d sq.
Bl. The K. Knight at his B. sq.

23.

Wh. Knight at the bl. Q. 4th sq. and must win.

FOURTH BACK GAME.

11.

Wh. The Queen takes the Bishop.
Bl. K. Knight *checks* at the wh. K. Kt. 4th.

(*b*) Any thing else, you must have taken his king's knight with your rook, and afterwards have given him check with your queen's rook to take his rook.

12.

Wh. The King at his Kt. sq.
Bl. The K. Kt. Pawn takes the Pawn (*a*)

13.

Wh. The Q. Bishop takes the Pawn.
Bl. The K. Knight at his B. 3d sq.

14.

Wh. The Knight at his Q. R. 3d sq.
Bl. The Queen takes the Queen.

15.

Wh. The Pawn takes the Queen.
Bl. The K. Knight at his R. 4th sq.

16.

Wh. The K. Rook takes the Pawn.
Bl. The K. Knight takes the Bishop.

17.

Wh. The Rook takes the Knight.
Bl. The K. B. Pawn one sq.

18.

Wh. The King at his B. 2d sq.
Bl. The King castles.

19.

Wh. The Bishop at the bl. K. 3d sq.
Bl. The Bishop at his K. 2d sq.

(*a*) If he had played any thing else, you must have taken the pawn with yours.

20.

Wh. The Q. Rook at its K. R. sq.

Bl. The King at his Q. Kt. sq.

21.

Wh. The Bishop takes the Knight.

Bl. The Rook takes the Bishop.

22.

Wh. The Q. Rook at the bl. K. R. 3d sq.

Bl. The Q. Kt. Pawn one sq.

23.

Wh. The K. Rook at the bl. K. B. 4th sq.

Bl. The Bishop at his Q. sq.

24.

Wh. The K. Rook at the bl. K. R. 4th sq.

Bl. The King at his Q. Kt. 2d sq.

25.

Wh. The K. B. Pawn one sq.

Bl. The Q. B. Pawn one sq.

26.

Wh. The K. B. Pawn one sq. (*b*).

(*b*) In this situation your adversary being unable to attack any of your pieces, your business is to bring your knight to the black king's knight's third square, in order to take his rook's pawn, which will give you the game.

THIRD GAMBIT,

WITH

THREE BACK GAMES.

1.

Wh. THE K. Pawn 2 sq.
Bl. The same.

2.

Wh. The K. B. Pawn 2 sq.
Bl. The Q. Pawn 2 sq. ☞

3.

Wh. The K. Pawn takes the Pawn.
Bl. The Queen takes the Pawn. ☞

4.

Wh. The B. Pawn takes the Pawn.
Bl. The Queen takes the Pawn, and *checks.*

5.

Wh. The Bishop covers the *check* (*a*)
Bl. The K. Bishop at his Q. 3d sq.

(*a*) In this situation the game appears equal on both sides. However, you have a small advantage, by having on your left wing four pawns, and that of your queen at

6.

Wh. The K. Knight at his B. 3d sq.
Bl. The Queen at her K. 2d sq.

7.

Wh. The Q. Pawn 2 sq.
Bl. The Q. Bishop at his K. 3d sq.

8.

Wh. The King castles.
Bl. The Q. Knight at his Q. 2d sq.

9.

Wh. The Q. B. Pawn 2 sq.
Bl. The Q. B. Pawn one sq.

10.

Wh. The Q. Knight at his B. 3d sq.
Bl. The K. Knight at his B. 3d sq.

11.

Wh. The K. Bishop at his Q. 3d sq.
Bl. The King castles with his Rook. ☞

12.

Wh. Q. Bishop at the bl. K. Kt. 4th sq. (*b*)
Bl. The K. R. Pawn one sq.

---

the head of them, whilst your adversary's are divided, three on each side, and separated from the centre. Therefore you are better able to hinder his pieces placing themselves in the middle of the board.

(*b*) Had he castled with his queen's rook, this would

13.

Wh. The Q. Bishop at his K. R. 4th sq.

Bl. The Queen at her home.

14.

Wh. The Q. Knight at his K. 4th sq. (*c*)

Bl. The K. Bishop at his K. 2d sq.

15.

Wh. The Queen at her K. 2d sq.

Bl. The Queen at her B. 2d sq. (*d*)

16.

Wh. The Q. Knight takes the Knight.

Bl. The Knight takes the Knight.

17.

Wh. The Bishop takes the Knight.

Bl. The Bishop takes the Bishop.

---

have been ill played; because you had lost a move by his pushing his rook's pawn upon your bishop, or you had been forced then to change it for his knight, which would have done you no good, because his other knight would have retaken his place. But you play it now to excite him to push his pawns that cover his king, that you may easier form your attack upon him.

(*c*) If he had not removed her to make room for his bishop, your knight would have been very troublesome to him.

(*d*) If he takes your knight, you must take it with your queen. This would puzzle him to save the threatened mate.

18.

Wh. The Queen at her K. 4th sq.

Bl. The K. Kt. Pawn one sq.

19.

Wh. The Knight at the bl. K. 4th sq.

Bl. The Bishop takes the Knight (*e*)

20.

Wh. The Pawn takes the Bishop.

Bl. The Q. Rook at its Q. sq. (*f*)

21.

Wh. The K. Rook at the bl. K. B. 3d sq.

Bl. The Queen at her 2d sq. (*g*)

22.

Wh. The Rook takes the bl. K. Kt. Pawn, and *checks*.

Bl. The Pawn takes the Rook.

23.

Wh. The Queen takes the Pawn and *checks*.

(*e*) Should he retire his bishop, you must take his king's knight's pawn with your knight, and that would give you the game.

(*f*) If he attacked your queen with his bishop, you must take his bishop with your king's rook. This would make an important opening upon his king.

(*g*) Had he not played the queen at that place, you must have taken his bishop with your rook, and you would infallibly have won the game.

Bl. The King at his R. sq. (*h*)

24.

Wh. The Queen takes the R. Pawn, and gives a perpetual *check.*

FIRST BACK GAME.

2.

Wh. The K. B. Pawn 2 sq.

Bl. The Q. Pawn one sq.

3.

Wh. The K. Knight at his B. 3d sq.

Bl. The Q. Bishop at the wh. K. Kt. 4th sq.

4.

Wh. The K. Bishop at his Q. B. 4th sq.

Bl. The Q: Knight at his B. 3d sq. (*a*)

(*h*) If he had covered it with his queen, you must have taken his bishop, giving him check, and you would have remained with a bishop and two pawns against his rook, besides a good attack, which was enough to win the game. As the party stands at present, it is not worth while to finish it.

(*a*) See Rule G. 1. Therefore, the black plays this knight at his bishop's third square, to defend his king's pawn, and to attack your king's bishop's pawn, which proves very incommodious to him upon that line. If he

5.

Wh. The Q. B. Pawn one sq.
Bl. The Bishop takes the Knight (*b*)

6.

Wh. The Queen takes the Bishop.
Bl. The K. Knight at his B. 3d sq.

7.

Wh. The Q. Pawn one sq.
Bl. The Q. Knight at his R. 4th sq.

8.

Wh. The K. Bishop *checks* at the bl. Q. Kt.
4th sq.
Bl. The Q. B. Pawn one sq.

9.

Wh. The K. Bishop at his Q. R. 4th sq.
Bl. The Q. Kt. Pawn 2 sq.

---

had played any thing else, you must have taken his
king's pawn with your king's bishop's pawn, and then,
giving him check with your king's bishop, your queen
would have taken his queen's bishop; but if he had taken
your king's bishop's pawn instead of playing his knight,
must have played your queen's pawn two squares, and
that would have made a gambit.

(*b*) Should he play any thing else without attacking
some of your pieces, you must play your queen at her
knight's third square. *Vide* the fifth back game of the
first gambit, couplet 8.

10.

Wh. The K. Bishop at his Q. B. 2d sq. (*c*)
Bl. The K. Bishop at his K. 2d sq.

11.

Wh. The Q. Pawn one sq.
Bl. The K. Pawn takes the Q. Pawn.

12.

Wh. The Q. B. Pawn takes the Pawn.
Bl. The King castles.

13.

Wh. The Q. Bishop at his K. 3d sq.
Bl. The Q. Knight at the wh. Q. B. 4th sq.

14.

Wh. The Q. Knight at his Q. 2d sq. (*d*)

(*c*) Without a true knowledge of the game, one would naturally conclude that these three last moves were, as they appear, not only lost moves, but also contrary to the many rules prescribed. Nevertheless, when you observe that he, in the chace, lost as many moves, and brought his game in such a situation that he cannot castle on his queen's side, without losing the game in a few moves, and taking his king's side for that purpose, your king's bishop is extremely well situated to attack his king, you will confess these three moves to have been well calculated; the more so, because your being now master of the middle part of the board, you may place your pawns as you please. If the centre is well sustained, the battle is half won.

(*d*) By thus playing, you leave one of your pawns ex-

Bl. Q. Knight takes the wh. Q. Kt. Pawn.

15.

Wh. The K. Kt. Pawn 2 sq. (*e*)

Bl. The Q. Knight at the wh. Q. B. 4th sq.

16.

Wh. The Knight takes the Knight.

Bl. The Pawn takes the Knight.

17.

Wh. The K. Kt. Pawn one sq.

Bl. The Knight at his Q. 2d sq.

18.

Wh. The K. R. Pawn 2 sq.

Bl. The Queen gives *check.*

19.

Wh. The King at his Q. sq.

Bl. The Queen at the wh. Q. R. 3d sq.

20.

Wh. The Q. Rook at its B. sq.

Bl. The Queen takes the R. Pawn.

---

posed to his knight, without an apparent necessity for it : see Rule A 10. Therefore you find your account better in pursuing your attack.

(*e*) This is played to dislodge afterwards his king's knight ; you might have done the same, pushing only your king's pawn : but in this case, he would have played it at his Queen's fourth square, which would have

21.

Wh. The Queen at the bl. K. R. 4th sq. (*f*)
Bl. The Q. Rook at its Kt. sq.

22.

Wh. The K. Pawn one sq.
Bl. The K. Kt. Pawn one sq.

23.

Wh. The Queen at her K. 2d sq.
Bl. The Q. Rook at the wh. Q. Kt. 2d sq.

24.

Wh. The K. R. Pawn one sq.
Bl. The Q. B. Pawn one sq. (*g*)

25.

Wh. The K. R. Pawn takes the Pawn.
Bl. The K. B. Pawn takes it. (*h*)

---

proved a great obstacle to your attack. In this circumstance you may see the utility of your front pawns,
because they will be able to force that knight to retire in
his trenches, and remain out of power to hurt you in the
whole course of the game.

(*f*) To oblige him to push his king's knight's pawn;
this will enable you to attack your adversary with your
rook's pawn, and make an opening upon his king, which
you will see.

(*g*) Or any other piece, the game being lost.

(*h*) In case he had taken with his rook's pawn, you
must have played your queen at your king's rook's se-

26.

Wh. The K. Rook takes the bl. K. R. Pawn.

Bl. The King takes the Rook (*i*)

27.

Wh. The Q. *checks* at the bl. K. R. 4th sq.

Bl. The King where he can.

28.

Wh. The Queen taking the Pawn gives *check,* and *Mate* the following move.

SECOND BACK GAME.

3.

Wh. The K. Pawn takes the Q. Pawn.

Bl. The K. Pawn takes the B. Pawn.

4.

Wh. The K. Knight at his B. 3d sq.

Bl. The Queen takes the Pawn.

---

cond square; which had won you the game equally. You may make the trial of it.

(*i*) If he had played his own at his king's bishop's second square, you must have retired yours one square, and sustained it afterwards with your queen. The mate would have appeared the same, and only prolonged one move or two more.

5.

Wh. The Q. Pawn 2 sq.

Bl. The Q. *checks* at the wh. K. 4th sq.

6.

Wh. The King at his B. 2d sq.

Bl. The K. Bishop at his K. 2d sq. (*a*)

7.

Wh. The K. Bishop at his Q. 3d sq.

Bl. The Queen at her B. 3d sq.

8.

Wh. The Q. Bishop takes the Pawn.

Bl. The Q. Bishop at her K. 3d sq.

9.

Wh. The Queen at her K. 2d sq.

Bl. The Queen at her 2d sq.

10.

Wh. The Q. B. Pawn 2 sq.

Bl. The Q. B. Pawn one sq.

11.

Wh. The Q. Knight at his B. 3d sq.

Bl. The K. Knight at his B. 3d sq.

(*a*) If he had not covered his king, and had left his queen where she was, he would have run the risk of losing her or the game soon after ; because you would have given check with your bishop, and afterwards your king's rook would have attacked her.

12.

Wh. The K. R. Pawn one sq.

Bl. The King castles.

13.

Wh. The K. Kt. Pawn 2 sq.

Bl. The K. Bishop at his Q. 3d sq.

14.

Wh. The K. Knight at the bl. K. 4th sq.

Bl. The Bishop takes the Knight.

15.

Wh. The Pawn takes the Bishop. (*b*)

Bl. The K. Knight at his K. sq.

16.

Wh. The Q. Rook at its Q. sq.

Bl. The Queen at her K. 2d sq.

17.

Wh. The K. Kt. Pawn one sq.

Bl. The Q. Knight at his Q. 2d sq.

18.

Wh. The Queen at the bl. K. R. 4th sq. (*c*)

Bl. The K. Kt. Pawn one sq.

(*b*) You take with your pawn to force his knight back, having no place to advance it ; you would not have removed him if you had attacked him with your bishop.

(*c*) See the letter (*f*) in the previous back game.

R

19.

Wh. The Queen at the bl. **K. R. 3d** sq.

Bl. The Queen gives *check.*

20.

Wh. The King at his Kt. 3d sq.

Bl. The Q. Knight takes the K. Pawn.

21.

Wh. The Knight at his K. 4th sq.

Bl. The Queen at the wh. Q. 4th sq. (*d*)

22.

Wh. The Knight *checks* at the bl. **K. B.** 3d sq.

Bl. The Knight takes the Knight.

23.

Wh. The Pawn takes the Knight and forces the *Mate.*

Bl. Lost.

THIRD BACK GAME.

11.

Wh. The K. Bishop at his Q. 3d sq.

Bl. The King castles on his Q. side.

(*d*) If he had played his queen any where else, he had lost his knight, and that would have been sufficient to lose the game.

12.

Wh. The K. Rook at its K. sq.

Bl. The Queen retires to her K. B. sq. (*a*)

13.

Wh. The Queen at her R. 4th sq.

Bl. The King at his Q. Kt. sq.

14.

Wh. The Q. Bishop at his K. 3d sq.

Bl. The Q. B. Pawn one sq. (*b*)

15.

Wh. The Q. Pawn one sq.

Bl. The Q. Bishop at the wh. K. Kt. 4th sq.

16.

Wh. The Q. Kt. Pawn 2 sq.

Bl. The Q. Bishop takes the Knight.

17.

Wh. The Pawn takes the Bishop.

Bl. The Q. Rook at its B. sq. (*c*)

(*a*) To avoid the loss of a piece, which you could force, by pushing your queen's pawn upon his queen's bishop.

(*b*) If he had attacked your queen with his queen's knight, you must have retired to her knight's third square, and afterwards pushed your rook's pawn to dislodge his knight.

(*c*) Any thing he can play, he cannot avoid losing the game, if it be well conducted on both sides.

18.

Wh. The Knight at the bl. Q. Kt. 4th sq.

Bl. The Q. R. Pawn one sq.

19.

Wh. The Knight takes the Bishop.

Bl. The Queen takes the Knight.

20.

Wh. The Q. Rook at its Kt. sq.

Bl. The Q. Knight at its K. 4th sq.

21.

Wh. The K. Bishop at his K. 2d sq.

Bl. The K. Knight at his Q. 2d sq.

22.

Wh. The Queen at the bl. Q. R. 4th sq.

Bl. The Queen *checks* at her K. Kt. 3d sq.

23.

Wh. The King at his R. sq.

Bl. The Queen at her 3d sq. (*d*)

24.

Wh. The Pawn takes the Pawn.

Bl. The K. Knight takes the Pawn.

25.

Wh. The Q. Rook at the bl. Q. Kt. 3d sq.

(*d*) If he had played any thing else, you must have taken his pawn with your queen's knight's pawn; and in case he had taken it, you must have taken with your rook, in order to double the rooks afterwards.

Bl. The Queen at her K. B. sq.

26.

Wh. The K. Rook at its Q. Kt. sq.

Bl. The Q. Knight at his Q. 2d sq.

27.

Wh. The Q. Rook takes the Q. R. Pawn.

Bl. The Knight takes the Rook.

28.

Wh. The Queen takes the Knight.

Bl. The Q. Rook at its B. 2d sq.

29.

Wh. The Q. Pawn one sq. and wins the game.

FOURTH GAMBIT,

WITH

TWO BACK GAMES,

COMMONLY CALLED

CUNNINGHAM'S GAMBIT.*

1.

Wh. THE K. Pawn 2 sq.
Bl. The same.

2.

Wh. The K. B. Pawn 2 sq.
Bl. The K. Pawn takes the Pawn.

3.

Wh. The K. Knight at his B. 3d sq.
Bl. The K. Bishop at his K. 2d sq.

4.

Wh. The K. Bishop at his Q. B. 4th sq.
Bl. The K. Bishop gives *check*.

---

* The author of this thought it a sure game, but I find quite the reverse ; three pawns well conducted, for the loss of a bishop only, will win the game, playing well on both sides.

5.

Wh. The K. Kt. Pawn one sq.*

Bl. The Pawn takes the Pawn.

6.

Wh. The King castles.

Bl. The Pawn takes the R. Pawn, and *checks.*

7.

Wh. The King at his R. sq.

Bl. The K. Bishop at his 3d sq. (*a*)

8.

Wh. The K. Pawn one sq.

Bl. The Q. Pawn 2 sq.

9.

Wh. The K. Pawn takes the Bishop. (*b*)

Bl. The K. Knight takes the Pawn.

---

* See the observation of Philidor on this move, at the end of the second back game.

(*a*) If he had played it at his king's second square, you had won the game in a few moves.

(*b*) Without a sacrifice of this bishop, he could not win the game; but, losing it, for three pawns, he must by a good management of them, become your conqueror. Those three pawns (provided he doth not be too hasty in pushing them forwards, and that they be always well sustained by his pieces) will win the game in spite of your best defence.

10.

Wh. The K. Bishop at his Q. Kt. 3d sq.

Bl. The Q. Bishop at his K. 3d sq.

11.

Wh. The Q. Pawn one sq. (*c*) ☜

Bl. The K. R. Pawn one sq. (*d*)

12.

Wh. The Q. Bishop at his K. B. 4th sq.

Bl. The Q. B. Pawn 2 sq.

13.

Wh. The Q. Bishop takes the Pawn next his King.

Bl. The Q. Knight at his B. 3d sq.

14.

Wh. The Q. Knight at his Q. 2d sq.

Bl. K. Knight at the wh. K. Kt. 4th sq. (*e*)

(*c*) If you had pushed this pawn two squares, you had given his knight a free entry, which would have lost you the party.

(*d*) This move is of great consequence to him, because it hinders you from attacking his king's knight with your queen's bishop, which would have enabled you to separate his pawns by changing one of your rook's for one of his knight's, and this would have turned the game in your favour.

(*e*) To take your queen's bishop, which would prove very incommodious to him in case he should castle on his queen's side : see Rule C. 12.

15.

Wh. The Q. at her K. 2d sq. (*f*)
Bl. The Knight takes the Bishop.

16.

Wh. The Queen takes the Knight.
Bl. The Queen at her K. sq. (*g*)

17.

Wh. The Queen takes the Queen (*h*)
Bl. The Rook takes the Queen.

18.

Wh. The Q. Rook at its K. sq.
Bl. The King at his Q. 2d sq.

19.

Wh. The K. Knight gives *check.*

(*f*) You play this, not knowing how to save your bi-shop without doing worse; for, if you had played the bishop at your king's bishop's fourth square, to hinder the check of his knight, he would have pushed his king's knight's pawn upon him, and would have made you lose the game immediately.

(*g*) If he had played his queen any where else, she would have been cramped; therefore he offers to ex-change, that in case you refuse he may place her at her third square, where she not only would have been safe, but extremely well posted.

(*h*) If you did not take his queen, your game would be still in a worse condition.

Bl. The Knight takes the Knight.

20.

Wh. The Q. Rook takes the Knight.

Bl. The King at his Q. 3d sq.

21.

Wh. The K. Rook at its K. sq.

Bl. The Q. Kt. Pawn 2 sq.

22.

Wh. The Q. B. Pawn one sq.

Bl. The Q. Rook at its K. sq.

23.

Wh. The Q. R. Pawn 2 sq.

Bl. The Q. R. Pawn one sq.

24.

Wh. The Knight at his K. B. 3d sq.

Bl. The K. Kt. Pawn 2 sq.

25.

Wh. The King at his K. 2d sq.

Bl. The K. B. Pawn one sq. (*i*)

26.

Wh. The Q. Rook at its K. 2d sq.

Bl. The K. R. Pawn one sq.

(*i*) If he had pushed this pawn two squares, you had gained his queen's pawn, taking it with your bishop. This would have mended your game very much.

27.

Wh. The Q. R. Pawn takes the Pawn.

Bl. The Pawn takes the Pawn.

28.

Wh. The K. Rook at its Q. R. sq.

Bl. The Q. Rook at her home (*k*)

29.

Wh. The K. Rook returns to its K. sq.

Bl. The Bishop at his Q. 2d sq.

30.

Wh. The Q. Pawn one sq.

Bl. The Q. B. Pawn one sq.

31.

Wh. The Bishop at his Q. B. 2d sq.

Bl. The K. R. Pawn one sq. (*l*)

32.

Wh. The K. Rook at his home.

Bl. The K. Rook at its 4th sq. (*m*)

(*k*) He proposes immediately to change one for the other: see Rule G. 14.

(*l*) To push afterwards his king's knight's pawn upon your knight, to force it from his post; but if he had pushed his knight's pawn before he played this, you must have posted your knight at your king's rook's fourth square, and by this means you would have stopped the progress of all his pawns.

(*m*) If he had given check with his rook's pawn, he

33.

Wh. The Q. Kt. Pawn one sq.

Bl. The Q. Rook at its K. R. sq.

34.

Wh. The Q. Kt. Pawn one sq.

Bl. The K. Kt. Pawn one sq.

35.

Wh. The Knight at his Q. 2d sq.

Bl. The K. Rook at its K. Kt. 4th sq.

36.

Wh. The K. Rook at its K. B. sq.

Bl. The K. Kt. Pawn one sq.

37.

Wh. The K. Rook takes the Pawn, and *checks.*

Bl. The King at his Q. B. 2d sq.

38.

Wh. The K. Rook at the bl. K. Kt. 3d sq.

Bl. The K. R. Pawn gives *check.*

39.

Wh. The King at his Kt. sq.

Bl. The K. Kt. Pawn one sq.

40.

Wh. The Rook takes the Rook.

Bl. The R. Pawn gives *check.*

---

would have played ill, and entirely against the instruction given in the first party.

41.

Wh. The King takes the Kt. Pawn.

Bl. The R. Pawn makes a Queen, and *checks.*

42.

Wh. The King at his B. 2d sq.

Bl. The Rook *checks* at its K. B. sa.

43.

Wh. The King at his 3d sq.

Bl. Queen *checks* at the wh..K. R. 3d sq.

44.

Wh. The Knight covers the *check* having no other way.

Bl. The Queen takes the Knight, and afterwards the Rook, and gives *mate* in 2 moves after.

FIRST BACK GAME.

7.

Wh. The King at his R. sq.

Bl. The Bishop at his K. 2d. sq.

8.

Wh. K. Bishop takes the Pawn, and *checks.*

Bl. The King takes the Bishop.

9.

Wh. The King Kt. at the bl. K. 4th sq. giving double *check.*

Bl. The King at his 3d sq. (*a*)

10.

Wh. The Queen *checks* at her K. Kt. 4th sq.

Bl. The King takes the Knight.

11.

Wh. The Queen *checks* at the bl. K. B. 4th sq.

Bl. The King at his Q. 3d sq.

12.

Wh. The Queen gives *checkmate* at the bl. Q. 4th sq.

A SEQUEL TO THE
FIRST BACK GAME,

In case your adversary refuses taking your Bishop with his King, at the eighth move.

8.

Wh. K. Bishop takes the Pawn and *checks.*

Bl. The King at his B. sq.

9.

Wh. The K. Knight at the bl. K. 4th sq.

Bl. The K. Knight at his K. B. 3d sq.

10.

Wh. The K. Bishop at his Q. Kt. 3d sq.

Bl. The Queen at her K. sq.

(*a*) Any where else he loses his queen.

11.

Wh. K. Knight at the bl. K. Bishop's 2d sq.

Bl. The Rook at her Kt. sq.

12.

Wh. The K. Pawn one sq.

Bl. The Q. Pawn 2 sq.

13.

Wh. The Pawn takes the Knight.

Bl. The Pawn takes the Pawn.

14.

Wh. The K. Bishop takes the Pawn.

Bl. The Q. Bishop at the wh. K. Kt. 4th sq.

15.

Wh. The Queen at her K. sq.

Bl. The Q. Bishop at her K. R. 4th sq.

16.

Wh. The Q. Pawn 2 sq. (*a*)

Bl. The Bishop takes the Knight.

17.

Wh. The Q. Bishop gives *check*.

Bl. The Rook covers the *check*.

18.

Wh. The Knight at his Q. B. 3d sq.

Bl. The Q. Bishop takes the K. Bishop.

(*a*) This piece is sacrificed only to shorten the game.

19.

Wh. The Knight takes the Bishop.

Bl. The Queen at her K. B. 2d sq.

20.

Wh. The Knight takes the Bishop.

Bl. The Queen takes the Knight.

21.

Wh. The Queen takes the Queen.

Bl. The King takes the Queen.

22.

Wh. The Bishop takes the Rook. (*b*)

SECOND BACK GAME.

11.

Wh. The Q. Pawn 2 sq.

Bl. The K. Knight at the wh. K. 4th sq.

12.

Wh. The Q. Bishop at his K. B. 4th sq.

Bl. The K. B. Pawn 2 sq.

13.

Wh. The Q. Knight at his Q. 2d sq. (*a*)

(*b*) With the superiority of a rook, besides a good situation, he will easily win the game.

(*a*) To tempt your adversary to take it; which if he did, he would play very ill: see Rule E. 3. By the re-

Bl. The Queen at her K. 2d sq.
14.
Wh. The Q. B. Pawn 2 sq.
Bl. The Q. B. Pawn one sq. (*b*)
15.
Wh. The Pawn takes the Pawn.
Bl. The Pawn takes the Pawn.
16.
Wh. The Q. Rook at its B. sq.
Bl. The Q. Knight at his B. 3d sq.
17.
Wh. The Q. Knight takes the Knight.
Bl. The K. B. Pawn takes the Knight.
18.
Wh. The Knight takes the bl. Pawn next to his king.
Bl. The King castles with his rook.

---

union, one of the pawns will probably either make a queen, or cost you a piece to hinder it.

(*b*) If he had taken your pawn, his game would have very much diminished in strength, because his knight would have been sustained but by one pawn instead of two; besides, he would have been forced to retire his king's knight when attacked, in order to preserve the pawn that sustained it.

S

19.

Wh. The Queen at her 2d sq.

Bl. The K. R. Pawn one sq.

20.

Wh. The Q. Rook at the bl. Q. B. 4th sq.

Bl. The Q. Rook at its Q. sq.

21.

Wh. The K. Bishop at his Q. R. 4th sq.

Bl. The K. Kt. Pawn 2 sq.

22.

Wh. The Q. Bishop at his K. 3d sq.

Bl. The Rook takes the Rook.

23.

Wh. The Knight takes the Rook.

Bl. The Queen at her 3d sq.

24.

Wh. The Queen at her K. R. 2d sq.

Bl. The King at his Kt. 2d sq.

25.

Wh. The Queen takes the Queen.

Bl. The Rook takes the Queen.

26.

Wh. The Q. R. Pawn one sq.

Bl. The King at his Kt. 3d sq.

27.

Wh. The Q. Kt. Pawn 2 sq.

Bl. The K. R. Pawn one sq.

28.

Wh. The Q. Kt. Pawn one sq.

Bl. The Knight at his K. 2d sq.

29.

Wh. The Rook at the bl. Q. B. 2d sq.

Bl. The Rook at its Q. 2d sq.

30.

Wh. The Rook takes the Rook. (*c*)

Bl. The Bishop takes the Rook.

31.

Wh. The King at his Kt. 2d sq.

Bl. The K. R. Pawn one sq.

32.

Wh. The Q. Bishop at his K. B. 2d sq.

Bl. The King at his R. 4th sq.

33.

Wh. The K. Bishop gives *check.*

Bl. The Bishop covers the *check.*

34.

Wh. The Bishop takes the Bishop.

Bl. The King takes the Bishop.

35.

Wh. The Knight *checks* at his K. 3d sq.

Bl. The King at the wh. K. B. 4th sq.

(*c*) If not it will be the same.

.36.

Wh. The King at his R. 3d sq.

Bl. The King at the wh. K. B. 3d sq.

37.

Wh. The Knight at his K. Kt. 4th sq.

Bl. The Knight at his K. B. 4th sq.

38.

Wh. The Bishop at his K. Kt. sq.

Bl. The K. Pawn one sq.

39.

Wh. The Q. R. Pawn one sq.

Bl. The K. Pawn one sq.

40.

Wh. The Bishop at his K. B. 2d sq.

Bl. The Knight takes the Q. Pawn, and afterwards wins the Game.

———

A NEW OBSERVATION

UPON THE

CUNNINGHAM GAMBIT.

The first Four Moves as before.

5.

Wh. The King at his B. sq. (*a*)

Bl. The Q. Pawn one sq.

———

(*a*) I have already shewn, that the attack of that gambit is far from being good, since the defence must win

6.

Wh. The Q. Pawn 2 sq.

Bl. The Queen at her K. B. 3d sq.

7.

Wh. The K. Pawn one sq.

Bl. The Q. Pawn takes the Pawn.

8.

Wh. The Q. Pawn takes the Pawn.

Bl. The Queen at her K. 2d sq.

9.

Wh. The Q. Bishop takes the Gambit's Pawn.

Bl. The Q. Bishop at the wh. K. Kt. 4th sq.

10.

Wh. The Q. Knight at his B. 3d sq.

Bl. The Q. B. Pawn one sq.

11.

Wh. The Q. Knight at his K. 4th sq. and must win the game.

---

every way when tolerably well performed ; three pawns well conducted cannot be less than equivalent to a piece : But the sure way to succeed in the attack is, when the check is given with the bishop at the fourth move, to remove your king to his own bishop's place, and not push the pawn as Cunningham directs. This makes it impossible for your adversary to preserve the gambit's pawn, which it will be always in your power to take, and to preserve continually the attack upon him.

THE

QUEEN'S GAMBIT,

OTHERWISE

THE GAMBIT OF ALEPPO,

WITH SIX BACK GAMES.

———

1.

Wh. T<small>HE</small> Q. Pawn 2 sq.
Bl. The same.

2.

Wh. The Q. B. Pawn 2 sq.
Bl. The Pawn takes the Pawn.

3.

Wh. The K. Pawn 2 sq. (*a*) ☞

———

(*a*) If you had pushed this pawn but one square, your adversary would have shut up your queen's bishop for at least half the game; this the first backgame will shew.

A certain author (otherwise a very good player, who delights chiefly in this queen's gambit) teaches to push this pawn only one square; but this will convince him and others that it is better to push it two; nevertheless, I will agree, that by pushing it only one, you may sometimes deceive a bad player, but this does not justify the move.

Bl. The same. (*b*) ♘
4.
Wh. The Q. Pawn one sq. (*c*) ♘
Bl. The K. B. Pawn 2 sq. (*d*)
5.
Wh. The Q. Knight at his B. 3d sq.
Bl. The K. Knight at his B. 3d sq.
6.
Wh. The K. B. Pawn one sq.
Bl. The K. Bishop at his Q. B. 4th sq.
7.
Wh. The Q. Knight at his R. 4th sq. (*e*) ♘

(*b*) Had he sustained the gambit's pawn, he had lost the game. This will be seen by a second back game. But if he had neither pushed this pawn, nor taken the gambit's pawn, you must have pushed your king's bishop's pawn two squares, and your game would have been in the best of situations, for having then three pawns in front.

(*c*) If you had taken his king's pawn, you had lost the advantage of the attack ; as see the third back game.

(*d*) If he had played any thing else, you must have pushed your king's bishop's pawn two squares; and then your pieces would have had entire liberty to attack.

(*e*) If, instead of playing your knight in order to take his king's bishop, or make him remove it from that line, (according to Rule G. 12) you had taken the gambit's pawn, you had lost the game again. This must be shewn by a fourth back game.

Bl.   The K. Bishop takes the K. Knight. (*f*)

8.

Wh.   The Rook takes the Bishop.

Bl.   The King castles (*g*) ♘

9.

Wh.   The Knight at his Q. B. 3d sq.

Bl.   The K. B. Pawn takes the Pawn.

10.

Wh.   The K. Bishop takes the Gambit's
      Pawn. (*h*) ♘

Bl.   The Pawn takes the K. B. Pawn.

11.

Wh.   The K. Kt. Pawn takes the Pawn (*i*)

(*f*) Had he played his bishop at your queen's fourth square, you must have attacked it with your king's knight, and taken it the next move.

(*g*) If he had pushed his queen's knight's pawn two squares in order to sustain his gambit's pawn, you will be convinced by a fifth back game that he had lost the party; and if instead of either of these two moves, he had chosen to take your king's pawn, your taking his pawn would have hindered him from taking yours again with his knight, because he would have lost the game by your afterwards giving him check with your queen.

(*h*) Should you take his king's bishop's pawn with yours, you would lose the game.

(*i*) In taking this pawn, you give an opening to your rook upon his king, and this pawn serves likewise for a

Bl. The Q. Bishop at his K. B. 4th sq.

12.

Wh. The Q. Bishop at his K. 3d sq.

Bl. The Q. Knight at his Q. 2d sq.

13.

Wh. The Queen at her 2d sq.

Bl. The Q. Knight at his 3d sq.

14.

Wh. The Q. Bishop takes the Knight.

Bl. The R. Pawn takes the Bishop.

15.

Wh. The King castles on his Queen's side.

Bl. The King at his R. sq.

16.

Wh. The K. Rook at the bl. K. Kt. 4th sq.

Bl. The K. Kt. Pawn one sq.

17.

Wh. The Queen at her K. 3d sq.

Bl. The Queen at her 3d sq.

18.

Wh. The Knight at his K. 4th sq.

Bl. The Bishop takes the Knight.

---

better guard to your king; it stops also the course of your adversary's knight; and though you have at present a pawn less, you have the best of the game by the situation.

19.

Wh. The Pawn takes the Bishop. (*k*)

Bl. The K. Rook at his K. sq.

20.

Wh. The King at his Q. Kt. sq.

Bl. The Queen at her B. 4th sq.

21.

Wh. The Queen takes the Queen.

Bl. The Pawn takes the Queen.

22.

Wh. The Q. Rook at its K. sq.

Bl. The King at his Kt. 2d sq.

23.

Wh. The King at his Q. B. 2d sq.

Bl. The K. R. Pawn one sq.

24.

Wh. The K. Rook at his Kt. 3d sq.

Bl. The Knight at his K. R. 4th sq.

25.

Wh. The K. Rook at the Q. Kt. 3d sq.

Bl. The Q. Kt. Pawn one sq.

26.

Wh. The Q. Pawn one sq. (*l*)

(*k*) And thereby joins his comrades.

(*l*) To make an opening for your rook and bishop.

Bl. The Pawn takes the Pawn.

27.

Wh. The K. Rook takes the Q. Kt. Pawn.

Bl. The Q. Rook at its Q. sq.

28.

Wh. The Q. Rook at its Q. sq.

Bl. The Knight at his K. B. 3d sq.

29.

Wh. The K. Rook gives *check.*

Bl. The King at his R. sq.

30.

Wh. The Bishop at the bl. Q. 4th sq. (*m*)

Bl. The Knight takes the Bishop.

31.

Wh. The Rook takes the Knight.

Bl. The K. Rook at its B. sq.

32.

Wh. The Q. Rook at its Q. 2d sq.

Bl. The K. Rook at the wh. K. B. 4th sq.

33.

Wh. The Q. Rook at its K. 2d sq.

Bl. The Q. Pawn one sq.

34.

Wh. The Pawn takes the Pawn.

Bl. The Q. Rook takes the Pawn.

(*m*) To hinder the adversary's pawns advancing.

35.

Wh. The K. Rook at the bl. K. 2d sq.

Bl. The K. Kt. Pawn one sq. (*n*)

36.

Wh. One of the Rooks takes the Pawn.

Bl. The Rook takes the Rook.

37.

Wh. The Rook takes the rook.

Bl. The Rook *checks* at the wh. K. B. 2d sq.

38.

Wh. The King at his Q. B. 3d sq.

Bl. The Rook takes the K. R. Pawn.

39.

Wh. The Q. R. Pawn 2 sq. (*o*)

Bl. The K. Kt. Pawn one sq.

40.

Wh. The R. Pawn one sq.

Bl. The Kt. Pawn one sq.

41.

Wh. The Rook at its K. sq.

Bl. The Kt. Pawn one sq.

(*n*) If he sustained the pawn, the game was lost.

(*o*) If you had taken his pawn with your rook, you had lost the game; because your king would have hindered your rook's coming in time to stop the passage of his knight's pawn. This may be seen by playing over the same moves.

'42.

Wh. The Rook at its K. Kt. sq.

Bl. The Rook gives *check.*

43.

Wh. The King at his Q. B. 4th sq.

Bl. The Rook at the wh. K. Kt. 3d sq.

44.

Wh. The R. Pawn one sq.

Bl. The Rook at its Kt. 2d sq.

45.

Wh. The King takes the Pawn.

Bl. The R. Pawn one sq.

46.

Wh. The King at the bl. Q. Kt. 3d sq.

Bl. The R. Pawn one sq.

47.

Wh. The R. Pawn one sq.

Bl. The Rook takes the Pawn. (*p*)

48.

Wh. The Rook takes the Pawn (*q*)

Bl. The Rook at its K. R. 2d sq.

(*p*) Should he not take your pawn, you must take his; and that would give you the game.

(*q*) If, instead of his pawn, you had taken his rook, you had lost the game: this is found with but little trouble by playing the moves over again.

49.

Wh. The Pawn 2 sq.

Bl. The Pawn one sq.

50.

Wh. The Rook at its K. R. 2d sq.

Bl. The King at his Kt. 2d sq.

51.

Wh. The Pawn one sq.

Bl. The King at his Kt. 3d sq.

52.

Wh. The King at the bl. Q. B. 3d sq.

Bl. The King at his Kt. 4th sq.

53.

Wh. The Pawn one sq.

Bl. The King at the wh. K. Kt. 4th sq.

54.

Wh. The Pawn one sq.

Bl. The Rook takes the Pawn, and playing afterwards his King upon the Rook, it must be a drawn game, because his Pawn will cost your Rook.

———

FIRST BACK GAME.

3.

Wh. The King Pawn one sq.

Bl. The K. B. Pawn 2 sq. (*a*)

———

(*a*) This must convince you, that it had been better to

4.

Wh. The K. Bishop takes the Pawn.

Bl. The K. Pawn one sq.

5.

Wh. The K. B. Pawn one sq.

Bl. The K. Knight at his B. 3d sq. (*b*)

6.

Wh. The Q. Knight at his B. 3d sq.

Bl. The Q. B. Pawn 2 sq.

7.

Wh. The K. Knight at his K. 2d sq.

Bl. The Q. Knight at his B. 3d sq.

8.

Wh. The King castles.

Bl. The K. Kt. Pawn 2 sq. (*c*)

9.

Wh. The Q. Pawn takes the Pawn (*d*)

Bl. The Queen takes the Queen.

---

push your king's pawn two squares, because his pawn hinders the union of your king's and queen's pawns in front.

(b) He plays this, and the next move also, to hinder your king's and queen's pawns uniting.

(c) In order to push that of his king's bishop's upon your king's pawn in case of need, which would entirely separate your best pawns.

(d) If you had advanced your pawn, he would have

10.

Wh. The Rook takes the Queen.
Bl. The K. Bishop takes the Pawn.

11.

Wh. The K. Kt. at his Q. 4th sq.
Bl. The King at his 2d sq.

12.

Wh. The Q. Knight at his R. 4th sq.
Bl. The K. Bishop at his Q. 3d sq.

13.

Wh. The K. Knight takes the Knight.
Bl. The Pawn takes the Knight.

14.

Wh. The K. B. Pawn one sq. (*e*)
Bl. The K. R. Pawn one sq.

15.

Wh. The Q. Bishop at his Q. 2d sq.
Bl. The Knight at his Q. 4th sq.

---

attacked your king's bishop with his queen's knight to
oblige you to give him check ; and in this case, by playing his king at his bishop's second square, he had gained
the move upon you, and a very good situation of game.

(*e*) To hinder your adversary putting three pawns
in front, which he would have performed by pushing only
his king's pawn.

16.

Wh. The K. Kt. Pawn one sq.

Bl. The Q. Bishop at his Q. 2d sq.

17.

Wh. The King at his B. 2d sq.

Bl. The Q. B. Pawn one sq.

18.

Wh. The Knight at his Q. B. 3d sq.

Bl. The Q. Bishop at his 3d sq.

19.

Wh. The Knight takes the Knight.

Bl. The Pawn takes the Knight.

20.

Wh. The K. Bishop at his K. 2d sq.

Bl. The Q. Rook at its K. Kt. sq.

21.

Wh. The Q. Bishop at his 3d sq.

Bl. The K. Kt. Pawn takes the Pawn.

22.

Wh. The Bishop takes the Rook. (*f*)

(*f*) If you had taken his pawn with your knight's
pawn, he would have pushed his queen's pawn upon
your bishop, and afterwards would have entered your
game with a check of his rook, sustained by his queen's
bishop ; and if you had taken this pawn with your king's
pawn, he might have done the same ; that would have
given him a very good game : see Rule A 13.

T

Bl. Pawn takes the K. Pawn, giving *check.*

23.

Wh. The King takes the Pawn.

Bl. The Rook takes the Bishop.

24.

Wh. The K. Bishop at his 3d sq.

Bl. The King at his 3d sq.

25.

Wh. The K. Rook at its Q. 2d sq.

Bl. The Q. Pawn gives *check.*

26.

Wh. The King at his B. 2d sq.

Bl. The Q. Bishop at the wh. K. 4th sq.

27.

Wh. The Q. Rook at its K. sq.

Bl. The King at his Q. 4th sq.

28.

Wh. The K. Rook at its K. 2d sq.

Bl. The Rook at its K. square.

29.

Wh. The K. Kt. Pawn one sq.

Bl. The Bishop takes the Bishop.

30.

Wh. The Rook takes the Rook.

Bl. The Pawn takes the Pawn.

31.

Wh. The K. R. Pawn one sq.

Bl. The Q. B. Pawn one sq.

32.

Wh. The K. Rook at the bl. K. R. sq.

Bl. The Q. Pawn one sq.

33.

Wh. The King at his 3d sq.

Bl. The K. Bishop *checks* at his Q. B. 4th sq.

34.

Wh. The King at his B. 4th sq. having no other place.

Bl. Q. Pawn one sq. and wins the game (*g*)

SECOND BACK GAME.

3.

Wh. The K. Pawn 2 sq.

Bl. The Q. Kt. Pawn 2 sq.

(*g*) I let your game be lost, only to shew the strength of two bishops against the rooks, particularly when the king is placed between two pawns. But if instead of employing your rooks against his pawns, you had, on the thirty-first move, played your rook at the black queen's square; on the thirty-second move brought your other rook at your adversary's king's second square; and on the thirty-third move sacrificed your first rook for his king's bishop; instead of losing, you had made it a drawn game.

T 2

4.

Wh. The Q. R. Pawn 2 sq. (*a*)
Bl. The Q. B. Pawn one sq.

5.

Wh. The Q. Kt. Pawn one sq.
Bl. The Gambit's Pawn takes the Pawn.

6.

Wh. The R. Pawn takes the Q. Kt. Pawn.
Bl. The Q. B. Pawn takes the Pawn.

7.

Wh. The K. B. takes the Pawn, and *checks.*
Bl. The Bishop covers the *check.*

8.

Wh. The Queen takes the Pawn.
Bl. The Bishop takes the Bishop.

9.

Wh. The Queen takes the Bishop, and *checks.*
Bl. The Queen covers the *check.*

10.

Wh. The Queen takes the Queen.
Bl. The Knight takes the Queen.

(*a*) It is of the same consequence in the attack of the queen's gambit, to separate the adversary's pawns on that side, as it is in the king's gambit's to separate them on the king's side.

11.
Wh. The K. B. Pawn 2 sq.
Bl. The K. Pawn one sq.

12.
Wh. The King at his 2d sq.
Bl. The K. B. Pawn 2 sq. (*b*)

13.
Wh. The K. Pawn one sq.
Bl. The. K. Knight at his K. 2d sq.

14.
Wh. The Q. Knight at his B. 3d sq.
Bl. The K. Knight at his Q. 4th sq. (*c*)

15.
Wh. The Knight takes the Knight.
Bl. The Pawn takes the Knight.

(*b*) By this, his scheme is to force you to push your king's pawn, in order to make your queen's pawn, now at the head, be left behind, and of no use to you. (*Vide* Ref. (*l*) in the third party, page 193). Nevertheless you must play it; but you will strive afterwards with the help of your pieces to change this your queen's pawn for his king's, and give by this means a free passage to your own king's pawn.

(*c*) He is forced to propose the changing of knights, though by this move he separates his pawns; because if he had played any thing else, you would have taken his rook's pawn, playing only your knight at the black queen's knight's fourth square.

16.

Wh. The Q. Bishop at his R. 3d sq.

Bl. The Bishop takes the Bishop.

17.

Wh. The Rook takes the Bishop.

Bl. The King at his 2d sq.

18.

Wh. The King at his B. 3d sq.

Bl. The K. Rook at its Q. Kt. sq.

19.

Wh. The Knight at his K. 2d sq.

Bl. The King at his 3d sq.

20.

Wh. The K. Rook at its Q. R. sq.

Bl. The K. Rook at its Q. Kt. 2d sq.

21.

Wh. The Q. Rook gives *check.*

Bl. The Knight covers the *check.*

22.

Wh. The K. Rook at the bl. Q. R. 4th sq.

Bl. The K. Kt. Pawn one sq.

23.

Wh. The Knight at his Q. B. 3d sq.

Bl. The Q. Rook at its Q. sq.

24.

Wh. The Q. Rook takes the R. Pawn.

Bl. The Rook takes the Rook.

25.

Wh. The Rook takes the Rook, and must win the Game, having a Pawn superior, and a Pawn past, which amounts to a Piece. (*d*)

THIRD BACK GAME.

4.

Wh. The Q. Pawn takes the Pawn.
Bl. The Queen takes the Queen.

5.

Wh. The King takes the Queen.
Bl. The Q. Bishop at his K. 3d sq.

6.

Wh. The K. B. Pawn 2 sq.
Bl. The K. Kt. Pawn one sq.

7.

Wh. The Q. Knight at his B. 3d sq.
Bl. The Q. Knight at his Q. 2d sq.

8.

Wh. The K. R. Pawn one sq.
Bl. The K. R. Pawn 2 sq.

(*d*) One may see by this back game, that a pawn, when separated from his fellows, will seldom or never make a fortune.

9.

Wh. The Q. Bishop at his K. 3d sq.
Bl. The King castles.

10.

Wh. The King at his Q. B. 2d sq.
Bl. The K. Bishop at his Q. B. 4th sq.

11.

Wh. The Bishop takes the Bishop.
Bl. The Knight takes the Bishop.

12.

Wh. The K. Knight at his B. 3d sq.
Bl. The Q. B. Pawn one sq.

13.

Wh. The K. Knight at the bl. K. Kt. 4th sq.
Bl. The Q. Kt. Pawn 2 sq.

14.

Wh. The K. Bishop at his K. 2d sq.
Bl. The K. Knight at his K. 2d sq.

15.

Wh. The Knight takes the Bishop.
Bl. The Pawn takes the Knight.

16.

Wh. The Q. R. Pawn 2 sq.
Bl. The Q. Knight at the wh. Q. Kt. 3d sq.

17.

Wh. The Q. Rook at its 2d sq.
Bl. The Q. R. Pawn one sq.

18.

Wh. The Q. R. Pawn takes the Pawn.
Bl. The Q. R. Pawn takes the Pawn.

19.

Wh. The Rook gives *check.*
Bl. The King at his Q. Kt. 2d sq.

20.

Wh. The Rook takes the Rook.
Bl. The Rook takes the Rook.

21.

Wh. The Rook at its Q. sq.
Bl. The Q. Knight *checks* at the wh. Q. 4th.

22.

Wh. The King at his Q. Kt. sq.
Bl. The King at his Q. Kt. 3d sq.

23.

Wh. The K. Kt. Pawn 2 sq.
Bl. The K. R. Pawn takes the Pawn.

24.

Wh. The Pawn takes the Pawn.
Bl. The Q. B. Pawn one sq.

25.

Wh. The K. Kt. Pawn one sq.
Bl. The K. Knight at his Q. B. 3d sq.

26.

Wh. The Bishop at his K. Kt. 4th sq.
Bl. The Q. Kt. Pawn one sq.

27.

Wh. The Knight at his K. 2d sq.

Bl. The K. Knight at his Q. R. 4th sq.

28.

Wh. The Knight takes the Knight.

Bl. The Pawn takes the Knight.

29.

Wh. The Bishop takes the Pawn.

Bl. The King at his Q. B. 4th sq.

30.

Wh. The K. B. Pawn one sq.

Bl. The Q. Pawn one sq.

31.

Wh. The K. B. Pawn takes the Pawn. (*a*)

Bl. The Knight at the wh. Q. Kt. 3d sq.

32.

Wh. The Pawn one sq.

Bl. Rook at its K. R. sq. to give *checkmate*.

33.

Wh. The Rook takes the Pawn.

Bl. The Rook gives *check*.

34.

Wh. The King retires.

Bl. The Rook gives *checkmate*, at the wh. Q. B. sq.

(*a*) To make a queen upon the white queen's square, where his bishop sustains the pawn.

FOURTH BACK GAME.

7.

Wh. K. Bishop takes the Gambit's Pawn.
Bl. The K. B. Pawn takes the Pawn.

8.

Wh. The K. B. Pawn takes the Pawn.
Bl. The K. Knight at the wh. K. Kt. 4th sq.

9.

Wh. The K. Knight at his R. 3d sq.
Bl. The Queen gives *check.*

10.

Wh. The King at his Q. 2d sq.
Bl. The K. Knight at the wh. K. 3d sq.

11.

Wh. The Queen at her K. 2d sq.
Bl. The Q. Bishop at the wh. K. Kt. 4th sq.

12.

Wh. The Queen at her 3d sq.
Bl. The K. Knight takes the K. Kt. Pawn.

13.

Wh. The K. Knight at his home.
Bl. Queen at the wh. K. sq. giving *check.*

14.

Wh. The King retires.
Bl. The K. Bishop takes the Knight, and
will easily win the Game.

FIFTH BACK GAME.

8.

Wh. The Rook takes the Bishop.
Bl. The Q. Kt. Pawn 2 sq.

9.

Wh. The Knight at the bl. Q. B. 4th sq.
Bl. The King castles.

10.

Wh. The Q. R. Pawn 2 sq.
Bl. The Q. Knight at his R. 3d sq.

11.

Wh. The Knight takes the Knight.
Bl. The Bishop takes the Knight.

12.

Wh. The R. Pawn takes the Pawn.
Bl. The Bishop takes the Pawn.

13.

Wh. The Q. Kt. Pawn one sq.
Bl. The K. B. Pawn takes the K. Pawn.

14.

Wh. The Q. Kt. Pawn takes the Pawn.
Bl. The Bishop at his Q. 2d sq.

15.

Wh. The Q. Bishop at the bl. K. Kt. 4th sq.
Bl. The Pawn takes the Pawn.

16.

Wh. The Pawn takes the Pawn.

Bl. The King at his R. sq.

17.

Wh. The K. Bishop at his Q. 3d sq.

Bl. The K. R. Pawn one sq.

18.

Wh. The K. R. Pawn 2 sq.

Bl. The R. Pawn takes the Q. Bishop.

19.

Wh. The Pawn takes the Pawn.

Bl. The Knight at his R. 4th sq.

20.

Wh. The Bishop at the bl. K. Kt. 3d sq.

Bl. The Knight at the wh. K. B. 4th sq.

21.

Wh. The Queen at her B. 2d sq.

Bl. Knight takes the B. to avoid the *mate.*

22.

Wh. The Queen takes the Knight.

Bl. The Bishop at his K. B. 4th sq.

23.

Wh. The Queen gives *check.*

Bl. The King retires.

24.

Wh. The K. Kt. Pawn one sq.

Bl. The Bishop takes the Pawn.

25.

Wh. The Queen takes the Bishop.

Bl. The Queen at her K. B. 3d sq.

26.

Wh. The Q. Rook at the bl. Q. R. 3d sq.

Bl. The Queen takes the Queen.

27.

Wh. The Q. Rook takes the Queen.

Bl. The K. Rook at its B. 2d sq.

28.

Wh. The King at his 2d sq.

Bl. The Q. R. Pawn 2 sq.

29.

Wh. The Q. Rook at the bl. K. 3d sq.

Bl. The R. Pawn one sq.

30.

Wh. The Q. Rook takes the Pawn.

Bl. The R. Pawn one sq.

31.

Wh. The K. Rook at its Q. R. sq.

Bl. The R. Pawn one sq.

32.

Wh. The Q. Rook at its K. 3d sq.

Bl. The K. Rook at its B. 3d sq.

33.

Wh. The King at his Q. 3d sq.

Bl. The Rook gives *check*.

34.

Wh. The King at his 4th sq.
Bl. The Rook takes the Rook.

35.

Wh. The King takes the Rook.
Bl. The Rook at its Q. R. 3d sq.

36.

Wh. The King at his Q. 4th sq.
Bl. The King at his B. 2d sq.

37.

Wh. The King at his Q. B. 3d sq.
Bl. The Rook gives *check*.

38.

Wh. The King at his Q. Kt. 4th sq.
Bl. The Rook takes the Pawn.

39.

Wh. The Rook takes the Pawn.
Bl. The King at his 2d sq.

40.

Wh. The Q. B. Pawn one sq.
Bl. The K. Kt. Pawn 2 sq.

41.

Wh. The Rook at the bl. Q. R. 2d sq.
Bl. The King at his Q. sq.

42.

Wh. The King at the bl. Q. Kt. 4th sq.
Bl. The K. Kt. Pawn one sq.

43.

Wh. The King at the bl. Q. B. 3d sq.
Bl. The Rook gives *check*.

44.

Wh. The Pawn covers the *check*.
Bl. The Pawn takes the Pawn.

45.

Wh. The Pawn takes the Pawn.
Bl. The King at his home.

46.

Wh. The Rook at the bl. K. Kt. 2d sq.
Bl. The Rook at its 3d sq.

47.

Wh. The King at the bl. Q. B. 2d sq. and
afterwards pushing his pawn, will
win the game.

SIXTH BACK GAME.

10.

Wh. The K. B. Pawn takes the Pawn.
Bl. The Knight takes the K. Pawn.

11.

Wh. The Knight takes the Knight.
Bl. The Queen gives *check*.

12.

Wh. The Knight at his K. Kt. 3d sq.

Bl. The Q. Bishop at the wh. K. Kt. 4th sq.

13.

Wh. The K. Bishop at his K. 2d sq. (*a*)

Bl. The Queen takes the R. Pawn.

14.

Wh. The K. Rook at its B. sq. (*b*)

Bl. The Queen takes the Knight and *checks.*

15.

Wh. The King at his Q. 2d sq.

Bl. The Q. Knight at his Q. 2d sq.

16.

Wh. The Rook takes the Rook (*c*).

Bl. The Rook takes the Rook.

17.

Wh. The Queen at her K. sq.

Bl. The Rook at the wh. K. B. 2d sq. and
wins the Game.

(*a*) Any thing you could have played could not hinder you from losing a piece.

(*b*) If you had played your king, he had won it sooner, playing only his rook at your king's bishop's second square.

(*c*) If you had taken his bishop, he would have given you check with his queen at your queen's third square, and mate by taking your rook the following move.

To give Checkmate with a Rook and a Bishop, against a Rook.

The situation in which the pieces are put is the most advantageous for the defending Rook ; but in case the defender doth not choose that retreat, it is not at all difficult to force his King at the extremity of the chess-board.

SITUATION.

White. The King at the bl. K. 3d sq.
The Rook upon the Q. B. line.
The Bishop at the bl. K. 4th sq.

Black. The King at his Home.
The Rook at its Q. 2d sq.

1.

Wh. The Rook gives *check.*
Bl. The Rook covers the *check.*

2.

Wh. The Rook at the bl. Q. B. 2d sq.
Bl. The Rook at the wh. Q. 2d sq.

3.

Wh. The Rook at the bl. Q. Kt. 2d sq.
Bl. The Rook at the wh. Q. sq.

4.

Wh. The Rook at the bl. K. Kt. 2d sq.

Bl. The Rook at the wh. K. B. sq. ☜

5.

Wh. The Bishop at his K. Kt. 3d sq.

Bl. The King at his B. sq. ☜

6.

Wh. The Rook at its K. Kt. 4th sq.

Bl. The King at his home.

7.

Wh. The Rook at its Q. B. 4th sq.

Bl. The Rook at the wh. Q. sq. ☜

8.

Wh. The Bishop at his K. R. 4th sq.

Bl. The King at his B. sq.

9.

Wh. The Bishop at the bl. K. B. 3d sq.

Bl. The Rook *checks* at the wh. K. sq.

10.

Wh. The Bishop covers the *check.*

Bl. The King at his Kt. sq.

11.

Wh. The Rook at the K. R. 4th sq. and gives
mate the following move.

FIRST VARIATION.

4.

Wh. The Rook at the bl. K. Kt. 2d sq.

Bl. The King at his B. sq.

5.

Wh. The Rook at the bl. K. R. 2d sq.

Bl. The Rook at the wh. K. Kt. sq.

6.

Wh. The Rook at the bl. Q. B. 2d sq.

Bl. The Rook *checks* at its K. Kt. 3d sq.

7.

Wh. The Bishop covers the *check.*

Bl. The King at his Kt. sq.

8.

Wh. The Rook gives *check.*

Bl. The King at his R. 2d sq.

9.

Wh. The Rook gives *checkmate* at the bl. K. R. sq.

SEQUEL to the FIRST VARIATION.

6.

Wh. The Rook at the bl. Q. B. 2d sq.

Bl. The King at his Kt. sq.

7.

Wh. The Rook *checks* at the Q. B. sq.

Bl. The King at his R. 2d sq.

8.

Wh. The Rook *checks* at the bl. K. R. sq.

Bl. The King at his Kt. 3d sq.

9.

Wh. The Rook *checks* at the bl. K. Kt. sq. and takes the bl. Rook for nothing.

SECOND VARIATION.

5.

Wh. The Bishop at his K. Kt. 3d sq.

Bl. The Rook at the wh. K. B. 3d sq.

6.

Wh. The Bishop at the bl. Q. 3d sq.

Bl. The Rook *checks* at the wh. K. 3d sq.

7.

Wh. The Bishop covers the *check*.

Bl. The Rook at the wh. K. B. 3d sq.

8.

Wh. The Rook *checks* at the bl. K. 2d sq.

Bl. The King at his Q. sq.

9.

Wh. The Rook at the bl. Q. Kt. 2d sq. and gives *mate* the following move, at the bl. Q. Kt. sq.

SEQUEL to the SECOND VARIATION.

8.

Wh. The Rook *checks* at the bl. K. 2d sq.

Bl. The King at his B. sq.

9.

Wh. The Rook at the bl. Q. B. 2d sq.

Bl. The King at his Kt. sq.

10.

Wh. The Rook *checks* at the bl. K. Kt. 2d.

Bl. The King at his B. sq.

11.

Wh. The Rook at his K. Kt. 4th sq.

Bl. The King at his sq.

12.

Wh. The Bishop at his K. B. 4th and wins.

THIRD VARIATION.

7.

Wh. The Rook at its Q. B. 4th sq.

Bl. The King at his B. sq.

8.

Wh. The Bishop at the bl. K. 4th sq.

Bl. The King at his Kt. sq.

9.

Wh. The Rook at its K. R. 4th sq. and gives
mate the following move, at the bl.
K. R. sq.

PHILIDOR'S LEGACY,

Referred to at Page 50.

SITUATIONS.

White. The King at his Q. Kt. sq.
The Queen at her B. 4th sq.
A Knight at the bl. K. R. 3d sq.
The 3 Pawns of the Q. B. Q. Kt.
and Q. R. at their proper places.

Black. The King at his R. sq.
The K. Rook at the wh. K. Kt. 3d sq.
The Q. Rook at his proper sq.
The two Pawns of the K. R. and K.
Kt. at their proper places.

The White begins, and may speedily win.
The Learner will find an explanation and a
few remarks hereon, in page 313.

OBSERVATIONS

ON THE

CONCLUSIONS OF GAMES,

Shewing what may Win or give Checkmate, and what not.

THESE MAY WIN, &c.

1. A single Pawn, if his King be before him.

2. Two Pawns against one in general, especially if an exchange, one for one, can be prevented.

3. A Pawn and any Piece whatsoever, except a Pawn on a Rook's file, with a Bishop going on a different colour to the corner house of that file: see Rule H. 5.

4. Two Bishops.

5. A Bishop and a Knight.

6. A Rook and a Bishop against a Rook.

7. A Queen against a Bishop and a Knight.

THESE CANNOT WIN, &c.

1. A single Pawn, if the adverse King be before it, and continue on the same file; see Rule H. 8.

2. Two Knights.

THESE CAUSE A DRAWN GAME.

1. A Rook against a Knight.
2. A Rook against a Bishop; see Rule H. 6.
3. A Rook and a Knight against a Rook.
4. A Rook and a Bishop against a Queen.
5. A Rook and a Knight against a Queen.
6. A Rook against a Bishop and 2 Pawns.
7. A Rook against a Knight and 2 Pawns; because in this and the preceding case the Rook cannot be prevented being sacrificed for the 2 Pawns.
8. A Queen against a Rook and 2 Pawns.

ELUCIDATION

OF

PHILIDOR's LEGACY, Page 311.

THE White gives *checkmate* at two moves: 1st, The Queen at the bl. K. Kt. sq. and upon her being taken by the Rook, (the King cannot take her for the Knight,) 2d, The Knight at the bl. K. B. 2d. giving *smothered mate*.

x

The Learner will see that the nicety of this trick consists in the danger the white King is in from the black Rook. If the players forego the mate, and add to the black party the Q. Bishop at his 3d sq. and the Q. Kt. Pawn at his proper place, they will find it afford an excellent study.

THE END.

The Reader is requested to supply the word " Pawn" in the second line of the second couplet, page 155. For any other more trifling errors the Editor craves his candid indulgence.

RUFF, Printer,
Cheltenham.